What Jesus Really Said

About the End of the World

DAVID B. CURRIE

What Jesus Really Said
About the End of the World

CATHOLIC
ANSWERS
PRESS
San Diego
2012

What Jesus Really Said About the End of the World
© 2012 by David B. Currie

Published by Catholic Answers, Inc.
2020 Gillespie Way
El Cajon, California 92020
1-888-291-8000 orders
619-387-0042 fax
catholic.com

Cover design by Devin Schadt
Interior design by Russell Design
Printed in the United States of America
ISBN 978-1-938983-10-8

All italics added for emphasis in citations from Scripture and ancient texts are the author's.

To the next generation:
Elizabetta, John, Adelina, Mark, and Michael.

I wish to acknowledge the support of my family,
particularly for their patience during the hours of writing:
Colleen, Mary, Daniel, Elisabeth, Alison,
Bradley, Stephen, Benjamin, Stephanie, Matthew,
Ann, Jonathan, and Kathleen.

I am also indebted to Swantina, Simon, and Todd
for their invaluable assistance on the manuscript.

To be persuasive we must be believable;
to be believable we must be credible;
to be credible we must be truthful.

—Edward R. Murrow

We do not err because truth is difficult to see.
It is visible at a glance.
We err because this is more comfortable.

—Alexander Solzhenitsyn

The diligent reading of Sacred Scripture accompanied
by prayer brings about that intimate dialogue in which
the person reading hears God who is speaking,
and in praying, responds to him with trusting openness of heart.
If it is effectively promoted, this practice will bring
to the Church—I am convinced of it—a new spiritual springtime.

—Pope Benedict XVI

Contents

ONE

This Generation Will Not Pass: Jesus' Big Mistake?

The college student across the table was only a freshman, but she certainly knew her own mind. Her parents had paid for twelve years of Catholic education, and now she had matriculated at a major Catholic university. Yet there she sat, doggedly attempting to convince those of us at the dining hall table that abortion and contraception were perfectly acceptable choices, even for a serious Catholic. She knew her position contradicted the teachings of Christ's Church. But she didn't think it mattered.

Why? She had been taught in her Catholic high school religion class that the early Church was wrong about the end of the world; in fact, that Jesus himself was the source of the mistake. She had been taught that Jesus believed he would return in glory within a generation of his own time and that his disciples had shared this false hope. Since Jesus had been mistaken about the end of the world, she reasoned, both he and his Church could just as easily be mistaken about other things.

I wish I could say that this true story is an isolated case. It is not. In fact, I am willing to wager that most Catholics have encountered the claim that caused this young student to question her faith—the claim that Jesus and the early Church fully expected his Second Coming within a very short period of time. Maybe you have heard it in a homily or in an RCIA class. Perhaps you have listened to a catechist teach that St. Paul, too, mistakenly predicted an imminent Second Coming and that his flawed eschatology calls into question the authority of his other teachings.

Such ideas have been around for centuries—reaching critical mass during the Enlightenment—but we don't have to look very far into the past to find prominent popularizers, Christian and skeptic alike, of the scandalous notion that Jesus was just plain wrong about his Second Coming.

Bertrand Russell

The first on our list, Bertrand Russell, was one of the leading logicians and mathematicians of the twentieth century, as well as one of its most notorious atheists. In his 1927 essay *Why I am Not a Christian*, Russell laid out his case for rejecting Christianity, which included the claim that Jesus had predicted the end of the world within a generation:

> (Jesus) certainly thought that His second coming would occur in clouds of glory before the death of all the people who were living at that time. There are a great many texts that prove that. . . . He believed that His second coming would happen during the lifetime of many then living. That was the belief of His earlier followers, and it was *the basis of a good deal of His moral teaching.*[1]

Notice that Russell—just like our young college student—linked Jesus' moral authority to his misguided end-of-the-world teaching. His argument can be summarized thusly:

---

1   Russell delivered this lecture on March 6, 1927, to the National Secular Society, South London Branch, at Battersea Town Hall. It is included in Bertrand Russell, *Why I Am Not a Christian and Other Essays on Religion and Related Subjects*, ed. Paul Edward (London: George Allen & Unwin, 1957). The essay is also available online, John R. Lenz (Bertrand Russell Society) 1996.

1. Jesus claimed to be divine and that he would gloriously return at the end of the world within a generation.
2. On that basis, Jesus made moral demands upon his followers.
3. Jesus lived in the first third of the first century; the world did not end by the close of the first century, so Jesus was wrong.
4. Therefore, Jesus could not be divine as claimed. Either he was a fraud or his followers perpetrated a hoax.
5. Therefore, his moral teachings are not infallible either. We can pick and choose from his moral teachings as we see fit.

On the surface, this argument sounds logical. For a Christian, it creates a conundrum. Can we agree with Russell's basic analysis and keep our faith? Can we affirm Christ's divinity yet admit he was fallible? Can we hold to the moral teaching of Jesus while admitting he was wrong on certain facts? Do we even want to?

Christian thinkers have strained themselves to answer these questions in the affirmative. Their two main approaches can be summed up in the writings of two other well-known modern figures.

Albert Schweitzer

This influential Lutheran minister-missionary-musician-philosopher-physician was a contemporary of Russell's. Like Russell, he believed that Jesus had predicted his own Second Coming within a generation. Schweitzer also wrote that the leaders of the early Church, too, wrongly believed Christ would return in the final eschaton[2] before they died.

---

2   *Eschaton* is a theological term that refers to the events surrounding the end of the world. Pope Benedict XVI has explicitly rejected Schweitzer's view as "the apocalyptic approach" to Jesus' message. Pope Benedict XVI, *Jesus of Nazareth: From the Baptism in the Jordan to the Transfiguration* (San Francisco, CA: Ignatius Press, 2008), 46-63, 187-190.

So what did Schweitzer conclude? That the Jesus of the Bible was a fabrication:

> The Jesus of Nazareth who came forward publicly as the Messiah, who preached the ethic of the kingdom of God, who founded the kingdom of heaven upon earth and died to give his work its final consecration, never existed.[3]

Schweitzer was an exemplar and a forerunner of liberal Protestantism. He wished to remain a Christian in some sense while rejecting the historical understanding of that word. But more traditional Christians, intent on holding to the truths about Jesus revealed in Scripture and passed down through history, have also wrestled with the apparent problem of Jesus' unfulfilled predictions.

C.S. Lewis

Perhaps the most famous such example was the twentieth-century Anglican apologist C.S. Lewis, whom most would consider to be an example of orthodox, "conservative" Protestantism. He did not agree often with Russell and Schweitzer, but on this one thing they were in accord: Jesus was wrong about the end of the world.

But Lewis believed that, despite this mistake, Jesus was still divine and his moral teachings are binding. In fact, Lewis defended Christianity more effectively than almost anyone else of his century. Yet he had a problem. Of Matthew 24:34 he wrote, "It is certainly the most embarrassing

---

3   Albert Schweitzer, *The Quest of the Historical Jesus*, trans. W. Montgomery, (London: A & C Black, 1910), 20, 398. Schweitzer cited Matthew 16:28, 23:36 and 24:34; Mark 9:1; and Luke 21:32 as problematic passages for Jesus. He cited St. Paul in I Thessalonians 4:17, I Corinthians 7:29, and Hebrews 1:2; St. Peter in I Peter 1:20, 4:7; and St. John in Revelation 22:20 as evidence of early Church belief in an imminent end of the world.

verse in the Bible."[4] Why? Because in it, Lewis believed, Jesus had predicted a quick end to the world:

> "For as the lightning comes from the east and shines as far as the west, so will be the coming of the Son of man. Wherever the body is, there the eagles will be gathered together. Immediately after the tribulation of those days the sun will be darkened, and the moon will not give its light, and the stars will fall from heaven, and the powers of the heavens will be shaken; then will appear the sign of the Son of man in heaven, and then all the tribes of the earth will mourn, and they will see the Son of man coming on the clouds of heaven with power and great glory; and he will send out his angels with a loud trumpet call, and they will gather his elect from the four winds, from one end of heaven to the other. From the fig tree learn its lesson: as soon as its branch becomes tender and puts forth its leaves, you know that summer is near. So also, when you see all these things, you know that he is near, at the very gates. Truly, I say to you, this generation will not pass away till all these things take place. Heaven and earth will pass away, but my words will not pass away" (Matt. 24:27–35).

The passage seems direct enough. Jesus clearly states, and then solemnly emphasizes, that before a generation passes the things he is describing will happen. It is a recognizable description of the end of the world: The stars fall from the sky and Christ arrives on clouds in glory.

So Lewis was left with a conflict. He clung to his faith: Jesus was the God-man revealed in Scripture. He affirmed

---

4   C.S. Lewis, *The Essential C.S. Lewis*, ed. Lyle W. Dorsett, (New York: Simon and Schuster, 1996) containing the 1960 essay entitled "World's Last Night," 385.

the moral teaching of Jesus. Yet, he concluded that in this case Jesus was somehow mistaken. Although my respect for Lewis's faith, intelligence, and grit is profound, I find his solution intrinsically flawed. He seems merely to have closed his eyes and ignored the contradiction inherent in his approach to this issue.

In this approach, Lewis resembles millions of other Christians who live with a contradiction. They keep their faith and morals mostly intact, yet accept that the claims of Jesus were wrong. Then they wonder why that approach doesn't appeal to others. Or, they marvel that some young people—such as our Catholic coed above—refuse to submit to the moral code taught by this fallible Christ. But if he is wrong—fallible like the rest of us—then why bother to trust him on any issue? The skeptics are actually more consistent!

Rapturists

There is another alternative to Lewis's conflict; one that has become popular in the last century among most fundamentalists and many evangelicals. They claim that the generation to which Jesus referred in this and other passages is really *our* generation.[5] For what Jesus really meant is that once the first of those prophesied events occurred (and in one way or another they claim that it has), the final eschaton would come within a generation.

If that doesn't satisfy you, they will offer three other alternatives: Maybe *generation* really means the Jewish race, or the human race, or even the faith of all Christians.[6]

---

5   This view can be found in the Scofield Reference Bible, books by Hal Lindsey and Tim LaHaye, and many other places. For extensive treatment of dispensational and end-time thought, see David B. Currie, *Rapture: The End-Times Error That Leaves the Bible Behind* (Manchester: Sophia Institute Press, 2003), 25-41.

6   Of these four views, Eusebius Pamphilius of Caesarea offered the first, St. Bede offered

We will speak of generational language in more detail later. But at this point, skip back a few paragraphs and re-read Jesus' words. A plain reading indicates that Jesus indeed meant the generation listening to him. The more one examines the surrounding context, the clearer it becomes. (Don't worry; the Greek original is no more forgiving of these misinterpretations.)

For better or worse, we are stuck with the fact that Jesus meant his own generation. And indeed, this has been the prevailing view of the Church for as far back as we can go. Origen in the second century, and Sts. Hilary of Poitiers and John Chrysostom in the fourth, each wrote that the "generation" to which Jesus referred had to be the one alive at that moment.[7]

It is perpetuating a fraud on the text itself to claim that Jesus was referring to a generation of people that would appear 2,000 years or more after his Passion. This has not stopped some from claiming it anyway.

False forecasts

In a way, this is understandable. The gift of faith makes us certain that Jesus was who he claimed to be. Instinctively, we understand that maintaining an inner conflict between predictive mistakes and moral certitude does not really satisfy. But what then to make of his end-times claims?

Throughout history, many opportunists have seized on this conundrum. Some of them surely believed their own er-

---

the second and third, Theophylact of Ohrid offered the fourth. All cited in Thomas Aquinas, *Catena Aurea: Golden Chain Commentary on the Four Gospels*, trans. John Henry Newman, (Oxford: Parker, 1843); Mark 13:28-32; and Luke 21:28-33. *Catena Aurea* is an exegetical anthology of the Gospels. St. Thomas collected excerpts from the earlier writers, stringing them together like a chain as a commentary. It provides a rich source for the Fathers' thoughts on any passage.

7   Cornelius à Lapide, *The Great Commentary of Cornelius à Lapide*, trans. Thomas Mossman, (London: Hodges, 1896); Matt. 24:34.

rors; others were frauds. I am no man's judge: It is not important at this point to separate the sincere from the mendacious.

Because people tried to understand the teaching of Jesus in isolation from Church authority, all types of end-time movements arose. Ever since the second century, Christianity has been plagued with groups that have predicted the end of the world. History is littered with those who have followed these men, only to be disillusioned after the inevitable disappointment.

The Bible tells us that predictions about the end of the world had begun even during the lifetimes of the apostles. St. John makes clear that there were some in his day who predicted Christ would return before all twelve apostles died.[8] Such predictions continued unabated through the centuries. Here are only a few of them:

- Montanisin, A.D. 156, taught that Christ would return momentarily to Papuza.
- Hippolytus predicted the end in A.D. 500, based on the dimensions of Noah's Ark.
- St. Gregory of Tours set a final date of A.D. 805.
- A great many predicted the end at the close of the first millennium. They referenced the ancient bishop St. Irenaeus, who believed that the world would last for 6,000 years and end in the year 1000.
- Joachim of Fiore predicted the end in 1260.
- Christopher Columbus believed Christ would return by the mid-1600s.
- John Napier (inventor of mathematical logarithms) predicted the end of the world between 1688 and 1700.
- A group of Catholic theologians placed the end of the

---

8   John 21:2-24. But note that St. John specifically debunked the theory as without merit.

world in the 1700s.[9]

- Martin Luther predicted the end no later than the mid-1800s—in the spring, mind you.
- Mormons, Millerites, and Jehovah's Witnesses were sure Christ would return during the nineteenth century.
- Billy Graham thought it would happen in the 1950s.
- The Darbyites (dispensationalists such as those at Dallas Theological Seminary and Moody Bible Institute) predicted the end by 1988.
- Many alarmists connected the expected Y2K catastrophe at the dawn of the year 2000 with the end of the world.
- Harold Camping told followers the end was coming in the fall of 2011.
- Although I am writing this before the end of 2012, I can assure you that there is no reason to worry about some modern interpreters' belief that the ancient Mayan calendar predicts the end in December 2012.
- Neither should you be concerned that "Great Tribulation" will start in 2012, leading to the end of the world in 2019, as Jack Van Impe, the persuasive radio and TV preacher, has predicted.[10]

On its surface, predicting the end of the world doesn't seem like the smartest strategy for building a following. Eventually the deadline comes, and something had better happen!

What about Jesus?

The question before us is much more important than the

---

9 They assumed that there would be as many Jubilee years as there had been years in Christ's earthly life. Lapide, *The Great Commentary*; Matthew 25:35.

10 My book *Rapture*, pages 5–23, has additional details on false predictions. Van Impe has repeatedly predicted the Rapture and Great Tribulation many places, but in 2010 he set a deadline of Dec. 31, 2012. See http://www.youtube.com/watch?v=JiQ58YUOai0&noredirect=1.

reputations of the men, both the sincere and the shysters, who predicted the date of the Second Coming. Our question is, was Jesus one of these false prophets? Was he indeed wrong about the end of the world? Is it possible that false prophecies about the end of the world have merely flowed logically from the original false prophet?

As we have seen, some intelligent people have certainly thought this was so. And this idea fits well the spirit of the age. In our present culture there is a climate of mistrust for the wisdom of anyone who has gone before. A fallible Jesus easily fits that mindset. People think, "Of course Jesus was mistaken about things. People of that day thought the world was flat. They believed the sun revolved around the earth. No one understood evolution or DNA sequencing. Anyone who trusts the authority of people so uninformed should have his head examined."

So, is the case closed? Does an honest investigation of the facts show that Jesus was mistaken about the end of the world? Was he simply a false prophet?

We have arrived at the purpose of this book. To answer the question of what Jesus said about the end of the world—and thus the question of his very authority—we will examine the important passages in which Jesus discussed the end of the world and his own return. We will draw on history, the riches of Catholic Tradition, and especially on the scriptural context derived from Old Testament prophecy. For the early Christians who heard Jesus' words were immersed in the Old Testament—its history, its language, and its style. If we don't keep this in mind, it can be easy for us to miss what they would have immediately understood.

Jesus employed the language of the Old Testament prophets to predict a terrible event. Yes, he gave his solemn word that this event would occur within the generation of his disciples. And this does all connect to the end of the world, which Jesus also clearly predicted: his Second Coming in glory and judgment at the final eschaton. But the case is not open and shut. The reality is more complex than Russell, Schweitzer, and even Lewis grasped, and indeed more than many Christians today realize. And rest assured, it reveals a Jesus who was neither fraudulent nor fictional nor just tragically wrong about one thing, but a prophet of truth and a divine, infallible authority.

TWO

When Will This Be:
Jesus Answers the First
Question in Matthew

We are on a quest to determine exactly what Jesus predicted concerning his Second Coming and the end of the world, especially in regard to any anticipated time frame. The most important passage on this topic is the Olivet Discourse.

This discourse occurs on the Mount of Olives, where Jesus is answering questions posed by his closest disciples. These questions were prompted by Christ's declaration that the Jerusalem temple buildings would be utterly destroyed.

Although the Olivet Discourse appears in all three synoptic Gospels, the most comprehensive presentation of this material is in Matthew. We will examine the Olivet Discourse in Matthew 24, using other passages to supplement and clarify the important issues. As St. Augustine tells us, comparing the Gospels can improve our understanding,[11] so to conclude our investigation we will take a tour through Luke 17 and 19—which, although they contain some similarities, are substantially different from Matthew 23-25.

---

11   "When [the different gospel accounts] are compared, they help to guide the understanding of the reader." St. Augustine, *The Works of Saint Augustine: A Translation for the 21st Century: Letters 156-210*, vol. 3, trans. Roland J. Teske (Hyde Park, NY: New City Press, 2004), Epistle 199, 340:25.

The setup

The setting for the Olivet Discourse actually begins in the prior chapter, Matthew 23. The center of biblical Judaism was the second temple: its liturgy and its priesthood. In that chapter Jesus condemns these leaders of Jerusalem for their failures. This follows the pattern of Jeremiah, who lived in the time of the first temple.[12] Jeremiah spoke "woe" on the failed "shepherds" of Solomon's temple, predicted their replacement with new leadership, and then declared that Jerusalem and its temple were doomed. That temple was subsequently destroyed by the Babylonians in 586 B.C.

Later in Matthew, Jesus will predict the destruction of the second temple's buildings; but like Jeremiah, here in 23:13-29 he first pronounces woes on the scribes and Pharisees—seven of them—calling them "blind guides," "blind fools," and "serpents." Since neither scribes nor Pharisees exist today, we can be sure that these condemnations were limited to these historical characters and not transferable to any group today, Jew or Gentile. And we can be thankful for that, as these seven woes are brutal in their force.

Interspersed with these woes Jesus describes why these leaders are so evil: They do evil in the name of religion. They emphasize the minutia of ritual at the expense of inner integrity. But most telling of all, they have persistently refused to accept the correction of God's messengers.[13] In fact, they and their ancestors have murdered those messengers,

---

12 Jer. 23:1-6, 34:2.
13 We must be careful not to be too smug when we read this about the Pharisees. As St. John Chrysostom preached, "Moreover, there are many in our days like the Pharisees, who take the greatest care of cleanliness and outward adorning . . . yet who fill their souls with worms and gore and an inexpressible stench; who fill them, I say, with wicked and absurd lusts." Or, in a more modern tone, "Christians even now, who scrupulously recite the rosary, and fast in honor of the Blessed Virgin, and withal are guilty at the same time of luxury, rapine, theft, etc." Lapide, *The Great Commentary*, Matthew 23:24-28.

the prophets. Jesus alludes to the history of the Old Testament without explanation. Those who heard him understood the reference to "the blood of innocent Abel to the blood of Zechariah the son of Barachiah" (Matt. 23:35).[14]

The mention of Abel is a reminder that brother can kill brother out of jealousy.[15] Jesus will die as a result of the jealousy of the Jewish leaders. Zechariah is particularly appropriate to mention.[16] As was common for Old Testament prophets, Zechariah acted out God's prophetic messages with his actions. Remember his name, because we will return to Zechariah shortly.

These seven woes stand in contrast to the nine "blessed" proclamations in the Sermon on the Mount. There, in Matthew 5, Jesus delineated the rules of the kingdom he had come to establish—a new kingdom of God that fulfilled the New Exodus predictions of the prophets. Now, with these woes, Jesus declares that the current leadership of the temple cult would not be part of his new kingdom leadership. With their bad behavior and faltering faith they had cut themselves off from the promises.

Day of reckoning

Of course, at the very moment the ultimate messenger of God is standing in their midst, they are plotting his death.

---

14   The precise identity of Zechariah has three possibilities. 1. The last prophet slain in the Hebrew Bible of the time (2 Chronicles 24:21). 2. The father of John the Baptist. 3. The minor prophet by that name. The best alternative is the third. Scripture never mentions his death, but rabbinic tradition attests to his martyrdom, as with Isaiah and Jeremiah. See Curtis Mitch and Edward Sri, *The Gospel of Matthew: Catholic Commentary on Sacred Scripture* (Grand Rapids: Baker Academic, 2010), 298.

15   St. John Chrysostom, cited in Aquinas, *Catena Aurea*, Matthew 24:32-36. It is common Old Testament parlance to refer to all sons of Jacob as brethren.

16   These two names are probably mentioned because they include a layman killed in a field and a priest killed in the temple, thus signifying all martyrs. Remigius of Auxerre, cited in Aquinas, *Catena Aurea*, Matthew 24:32-26.

This time they are rejecting not just a messenger but the Son. Jesus declares that—finally—this ultimate rejection of God and his message will be punished. In Matthew 23:36 he proclaims that "all this will come upon this generation."

What does Jesus mean by "all" in this verse? The verses just prior describe examples of Jewish rejection and mistreatment of God's messengers. For generations, the leaders of Jerusalem had turned their backs on God's message. But except for the Babylonian Exile—which in Christ's time was a distant memory—nothing catastrophic had ever come of this rebellion against God. Now Jesus predicts the ultimate day of accounting for these scribes and Pharisees. It will come in their generation—the same generation that is even now plotting his demise.[17]

Jesus will use identical language concerning this "generation" later in the Olivet Discourse. At this point it is clear that he is referring to the generation of leaders that he has just condemned seven times. They are the ones who will personally face judgment.

Some helpful history

What happens? Are these hypocritical leaders punished as Jesus predicts?

Events will develop in dramatic fashion. This confrontation between Jesus and the Pharisees occurs in early April of A.D. 30. The Jewish leadership is at the height of its influence with Rome. No one but Jesus can imagine this, but in less than four decades—in the year 66—Jerusalem will revolt against Rome and set up an independent state. In that year the Jewish radi-

---

17   "This word *woe*, which is prefixed to intolerable pain, applies to those who were soon afterwards to be destroyed by dreadful punishments." St. Basil, quoted in Lapide, *The Great Commentary*, Matthew 23:13.

cals—called Zealots—will invade their own temple. They will overpower the temple guard, kill the Jewish high priest Ananias, and burn his palace along with all debt and slave records.[18] In their view, Ananias is a shill of Rome, an embodiment of injustice. Then the Zealots will stick a thumb in the eye of Rome itself, putting an end to the daily sacrifices being offered in the temple for the health of Caesar Nero.

In response to this, the Roman general Cestius will march on Jerusalem, burning much of the city. During the battle, the Roman army will fight its way right up to the gates of the temple. But, with victory almost in his grasp, Cestius will inexplicably break off the attack and embark on a risky retreat across the Judean countryside with the Jews in hot pursuit. Soon the retreat will become a disastrous rout, and Cestius will lose 6,000 soldiers and a greater portion of his war materiel.

As a result, the Roman garrison will become an island in a hostile sea. The Zealots will promise safe conduct to the Roman soldiers provided they first surrender their weapons. But upon laying their weapons aside and exiting their garrison, they will be ruthlessly slaughtered. The Roman ruler's palace will be torched for good measure. This expulsion of the Roman overlords will leave Jerusalem with the impression that God will continue to protect his temple. They will dare to think the unthinkable: They can defeat Rome when it comes to all-out war.[19]

Caesar Nero will be outraged. By February of 67, he will declare war against Jerusalem, dispatching the eminently competent Vespasian at the head of a massive Roman army. The

---

18   Josephus, *Wars of the Jews, The Life and Works of Flavius Josephus*, trans. William Whiston, (Peabody, MA: Hendrickson, nd), 2, 427. They might have been attempting a Jubilee declaration, but it was not the right year. The closest *shemittah* year would have been A.D. 68. We will discuss this later.

19   Josephus, *Wars of the Jews*, 2, 17-19.

Jewish-Roman War will rage for the next three and a half years. By June of 68, Vespasian will have Jerusalem surrounded, cut off from all aid or escape. But before he can finish the job, Rome will have had its fill of Nero. The army—even the palace (Praetorian) guard—will rise up in rebellion. Nero will flee Rome and commit suicide. Vespasian will leave Jerusalem unconquered because he then will have bigger fish to fry. He will return with his army to Rome, where he will successfully fight to establish his claim to the throne.

As Caesar, Vespasian will send his son Titus to finish the job Vespasian had started under Nero. By April of 70, Titus will have tightened the noose of the final siege of Jerusalem. In August the temple will fall to the Roman army and be torched. Within a month, the entire city will be under Roman control.

Jesus' improbable-sounding pronouncement of woe upon the Jewish leaders will indeed come to pass. Almost without exception, the leadership of Jerusalem will not survive; they will be killed by fellow Jews or by the Romans. In fact, about a third of the entire city will die (from infighting and starvation) before the Romans even enter Jerusalem; another third will be killed by the sword; while the rest will go into exile or slavery.[20]

That generation will reap "all" that they are sowing, and the prospect breaks Christ's heart. But rejection of God entails consequences.

Two judgments

About now, you might be saying to yourself: "I thought we were looking at the statements of Jesus concerning the end of the world and its judgment. What is this talk of Jerusalem's judgment?"

---

20   This is a reflection of Ezekiel 5:1-2, and just as Rev. 16:19 will predict. See Currie, *Rapture*, 318-320.

And there is the crux of the conundrum. As we will short-ly see, Jesus is actually going to talk about both events—the judgment at the end of the world and the judgment upon Jerusalem—within the Olivet Discourse. Therefore, it is in-cumbent upon us to determine when he is speaking of one event or the other, or both—or whether he simply mixes up the answers with no apparent reason.

Embedded within the passage are two structural clues that will guide our study. They are not structures com-monly used today in literature, but they were common in ancient times. Without them, the Olivet Discourse can seem a jumbled mess.

Clue number one

The first of these structural clues is the *inclusio*. This was a technique used by ancient teachers that employs the repeti-tion of an exact phrase to "bracket" a subject. Within the inclusio, the topic of the address will remain on theme.

For example, in the Sermon on the Mount, after Jesus enunciates the Beatitudes, the main portion of his teaching is bracketed by the phrase "Law and the Prophets" (cf. Matt. 5:17-7:12). The topic is unified between these phrases. An-other well-known inclusio can be found in Mark's Gospel. Peter is the first and last disciple mentioned in Mark, which is widely understood to be Mark's way of signaling that ev-erything in his book is from the eyewitness account of Peter.

Here in the Olivet Discourse, Jesus mentions "this gen-eration" twice. We already saw the first in 23:36, where he singled out the generation of Pharisees that was opposing his message. Jesus returns to those identical words—"this generation"—in 24:34.[21]

---

21   Evident also in Greek: panta epi ten genean tauten parallels panta tauta genetai.

This double mention is extremely significant, for without it we can become easily confused. The inclusio in Matthew stands as a signpost: The main subject will not change from the first mention of "this generation" until the second mention of "this generation." The unity of the inclusio is obscured in our Bibles because it is split in two by a chapter division that was added centuries later, but an ancient reader would recognize that there should be only one topic covered from the beginning of the inclusio to its end—from 23:36 to 24:34. To remain faithful to Matthew's intention and to understand the answers that Jesus gives in this passage, we, too, must remain aware of this inclusio until we get past verse 24:34.

Clue number two

There is another structural clue we must not miss. The preaching included within this inclusio is structured according to another common ancient literary device: a *chiasm*.[22] Prior to the easy availability of the written word, it was critical that important moral teachings be easily remembered,[23] and chiastic structures were used as mnemonic aids that would also emphasize important topics in a discourse.

A modern author tends to build to his climax point by point (A, B, C, climax) and then end shortly after the climax. In a chiasm, the author also arranges his topics building up to the climax (A, B, C, climax). But he repeats the topics in reverse order *after* the climax, thus forming a symmetrical structure (A, B, C, climax, C', B', A').

So, if a modern passage is like the Washington Monument—floor upon floor ascending until the climax of the

---

22   The structure can also be labeled a *palistrophe*, but we will use the term *chiasm*.

23   The ancients had an ability to remember details that would boggle modern minds. For example, Cyrus, who ruled Persia when it conquered Babylon, reportedly knew the name of every man in his vast army.

windows is reached at the top—then a chiastic passage resembles the Gateway Arch. The climax of windows is still at the top, but the floors ascend and descend in perfect symmetry on either side of the climax.

Think of a chiasm as a stepladder for ideas. Each side of the ladder has the same number of steps (topics), and the top step (climax) connects the two sides. The topics of a chiasm begin with A and progress through the alphabet up the ladder before climaxing in Z: the central teaching. Then the chiasm descends the other side of the ladder from the climax at the top, each topic repeating itself on the way down before concluding with A'. Unlike an inclusio, the chiasm does not need to repeat exact phrases, but the corresponding sections do use similar or even contrasting ideas. Special attention should be given to the climax, the core point of any chiastic address.[24]

Putting the clues together

These two structural signposts allow us to navigate this passage with accuracy. The chiasm in the Olivet Discourse passage can be arranged as follows, with the phrase denoting the inclusio—"this generation"—beginning in A and ending in A'. Everything in the inclusio from A to A' will be about "this generation." Here is an outline, but it would be worthwhile to turn to Appendix A and read the entire chiasm there.

---

24   Not every chiasm has a climax. Sometimes chiasms simply express a symmetry of ideas. For example, Isaiah 6:10:

(A) Make the *heart* of this people fat,
  (B) and make their *ears* heavy,
    (C) and shut their *eyes*;
    (C') lest they see with their *eyes*,
  (B') and hear with their *ears*,
(A') and understand with their *heart*, and convert [return], and be healed.

A   This generation (23:36)
 B   Gathering rejected (23:37)
  C   See the Son of Man (23:38-39)
   D   Going away (24:1a)
    E   Thrown down (24:1b-2)
     F   Knowledge sought (24:3a)
      G   Sign of coming (24:3b)
       H   False messiahs (24:4-5)
        I   Time of suffering protracted (24:6-8)
         J   Tribulation (24:9)
          K   Do not fall away (24:10-11)
           L   Wickedness (24:12)
            M   The end (24:13)
             Z   Preach the gospel of the kingdom (24:14)
            M'   The end (24:14b)
           L'   Sacrilege (24:15)
          K'   Flee! (24:16-20)
         J'   Tribulation (24:21)
        I'   Time of suffering shortened (24:22)
       H'   False messiahs (24:23-26)
      G'   Lightning sign (24:27)
     F'   Knowledge denied (24:28)
    E'   Falling (24:29)
   D'   Appearing (24:30a)
  C'   See the Son of Man (24:30b)
 B'   Gathering successful (24:31)
A'   This generation (24:32-34)

The Olivet Discourse continues after the chiasm ends
with A'. But since the end of the chiasm corresponds to the
end of the inclusio, the subject matter changes once we pass
the second mention of "this generation."

We have already examined the first topic of the chiasm:

segment A, which contains the warning to "this genera-tion." Let us move on to the other topics in order, and see if we can understand these words of Jesus that make skeptics scoff and believers blush.

A B C D E F G H I J K L M Z M' L' K' J' I' H' G' F' E' D' C' B' A'

Gathering rejected (23:37)

"O Jerusalem, Jerusalem, killing the prophets and stoning those who are sent to you! How often would I have gathered your children together as a hen gathers her brood under her wings, and you would not!"

At the start of this section, the tone of Jesus changes abrupt-ly and dramatically from the harsh "woes" that precede it. Before, he was speaking judgment against the proud and hypocritical religious leaders who claimed to know what was right and true. But the impending judgment on Jerusa-lem's leaders would also entail the destruction of the city and people Jesus loved, and this broke his heart. Jerusalem was the place of his Father's name.[25] Jerusalem had been witness to the truth of the prophets throughout salvation history. Jesus will not alter Jerusalem's fate, yet he cannot help but cry out in grief as he considers it.[26]

Throughout salvation history, God had spared nothing, not even his Son. But he would not force his will on his creation. God shows mercy without end and forgives every true penitent. But he will never trample upon our freedom. So when Jerusalem said, "We will not serve!"—when the

---

25 God identified himself with Jerusalem in this way. See 1 Kings 11:36; 2 Kings 21:4, 7; 2 Chronicles 6:6; 33:4.

26 St. John Chrysostom, cited in Aquinas, *Catena Aurea*, Matthew 24:37-39.

chosen people would not be gathered—God allowed them their way.

There is another group of God's people that Christ will successfully "gather" later. We will learn about them in segment B'. So B and B' are linked by the theme of gatherings—one unsuccessful and the other successful.

Luke makes explicit the connection between Jewish rejection of God and the coming desolation even more than Matthew does. When the leadership of Jerusalem rejected their Messiah, there was nothing left to protect them from God's judgment:

> When [Jesus] . . . saw the city he wept over it, saying . . . "[T]he days shall come upon you, when your enemies will cast up a bank about you and surround you . . . and they will not leave one stone upon another in you; *because you did not know the time of your visitation*" (Luke 19:41-44).

Jesus is torn between his affection for Jerusalem and his knowledge of its impending destruction. Jerusalem had rejected its only hope of salvation by rejecting the Messiah. From rejection will flow the logical consequence.

A B C D E F G H I J K L M Z M' L' K' J' I' H' G' F' E' D' C' B' A'

See the Son of Man (23:38-39)

"Behold, your house is forsaken and desolate.
For I tell you, you will not see me again, until you say,
'Blessed is he who comes in the name of the Lord.'"

This is a clear allusion to Jeremiah's prediction of the destruction of the first temple. Through him, God declared, "I have forsaken my house, I have abandoned my heritage; I have given the beloved of my heart into the hands of her enemies" (Jer. 12:7). Here Jesus speaks the same words against the second temple. The similarity of language should have caused chills to run down the spines of those who heard him. The destruction of the second temple will follow the pattern established when Solomon's first temple was destroyed.

Jesus turns away and pledges never to be seen in the temple until the leaders of Jerusalem say, "Blessed is he who comes in the name of the Lord." Hosea had written of this Israelite rhythm of rejection and repentance.[27] Now Jesus applies that pattern to his own relationship with Israel.[28]

In just a few hours Jesus will die on his cross, and then all Jerusalem will see that God's glory had forsaken the temple. At the moment Jesus dies, the veil that guarded the entrance to the Holy of Holies in the temple will be mysteriously rent asunder: God will have removed his name and protection, leaving the Holy of Holies empty, desolate, forsaken. The judgment that comes flowed from this reality. His chosen people's leaders had rejected him, so Jesus leaves them to their own resources; and the result is not going to be pretty.

Near the end of the chiasm, in the corresponding C', the subject of "seeing Christ" will be revisited. But the "seeing" in C' will be different. The first "seeing" in C results from blessing. It will be a joyous occasion similar to the triumphal entry into Jerusalem just days before this discourse. Then the Galilean Jews were shouting, "Hosanna to the Son of David! Blessed is he who comes in the name of the Lord! Hosanna

---

27   "For the children of Israel shall dwell many days . . . without sacrifice . . . without ephod or teraphim. Afterward the children of Israel shall return and seek the LORD their God, and David their king; and they shall come in fear to the LORD and to his goodness in the latter days" (Hos. 3:4-5).

28   Some do not take this as strictly predictive but rather as a conditional statement (Curtis Mitch, *The Gospel of Matthew*), 300.

in the highest!" (Matt. 21:9). Another day will come when Jerusalem's Jews will join in joyous shouts acknowledging Jesus as the Messiah. We know this will not happen until the Second Advent, but Jesus does not specify that here.[29] He leaves the option of repentance open even now.

The "seeing" in C', however, speaks of a day when Jerusalem will "see the Son of man coming on the clouds of heaven." Rather than uttering a blessing, at this "seeing" they will mourn. We will discuss that segment in much more detail when we get there, for it is the crux of Russell's skepticism and Lewis's embarrassment. *Did Jesus come as he promised?*

For now, in segment C, Jesus makes clear that he is forsaking Jerusalem and her temple. There will come a day when Jerusalem will bless him on his return, but this day of blessing has not yet come.

A B C D E F G H I J K L M Z M' L' K' J' I' H' G' F' E' D' C' B' A'

Going Away (24:1a)

"Jesus left the temple and was going away."

At this point, Jesus does the only logical thing left to do. He has denounced the leadership—the "false shepherds"—of his people, so he leaves. When man rejects God, God does not force himself on man. Since the majority of the religious leadership of Judaism rejected Christ, he left. What else was there to do?

Matthew lays out the narrative to reflect the experience of Zechariah, the martyr-prophet whom Jesus mentioned while condemning the Jewish leaders a few verses earlier, in Matthew 23:35. God commanded Zechariah to take a job as

---

29   "In this He covertly alludes to His second coming, when surely they shall worship Him." St. John Chrysostom, quoted in Aquinas, *Catena Aurea*, Matthew 24:37-39.

a shepherd. His fellow shepherds were evil men who cared
not a whit for the sheep. So Zechariah "destroyed" the evil
shepherds. But the sheep themselves "detested" Zechariah,
even though they knew he spoke for God. So he said to the
sheep, "I will not be your shepherd. What is to die, let it
die." With that, Zechariah broke his staff, "annulling the
covenant." Zechariah was bought off with "thirty shekels of
silver," which were subsequently "cast . . . into the treasury"
(cf. Zech. 11:7-14). Jesus is alluding to the tradition that
Zechariah was martyred by the Jewish leaders of his day.

This should sound familiar. Jesus has just finished verbally
"destroying" the leadership of Judaism. Now with his exit, he
is abandoning the sheep to "die" just as Zechariah had done.
Shortly after Jesus finishes this discourse, he will be sold out
for thirty pieces of silver. In the next chapter of Matthew,
Jesus will be killed. The false shepherds will be destroyed, as
they were in Zechariah's story. The pattern was laid out in
Zechariah, and Matthew knew it was a type of Jesus.

Matthew is also reflecting the scene that Ezekiel witnessed
just before the Babylonians destroyed the first temple. Ezekiel
saw a vision of the presence of God leaving the temple by the
east gate and resting on the Mount of Olives (cf. Ezek. 10:15-
22). In Jesus' day, God is once again leaving the temple, and
we will soon learn that he, too, goes to the Mount of Olives.

The sad aspect of this is that no one stops Jesus as he leaves.
In Zechariah's story, those who heard him knew that God
was speaking through him. Zechariah says that "the sheep,
who were watching me, knew that it was the word of the
Lord" (Zech. 11:11). When Jesus denounces the Jewish leaders in the seven woes, it is hard to believe that no one knows
he is speaking the truth of God. He is denouncing selfish,
evil shepherds, just as Zechariah had. Yet no one yells out,
"Wait!" as the Son of Man leaves the earthly throne of his

Father to its fate. With him goes any hope of their survival. The temple's doom is a *fait accompli*.[30]

On an eternal level, that is what hell is: the total absence of God. Man is left to his own fate without God's love and grace. It is a truly miserable existence. But like the Jews of Jesus' day, we sometimes blithely head down the road toward the absence of God with nary a thought of caution. St. Ambrose reminded us, "There is also a temple in every one, which falls when faith is lacking."[31] Each man is the cause of his own abandonment by God, in at least equal measure to that of the ancient Jewish leaders.

The leaving of Jesus in segment D follows closely on the heels of the prediction of a future "coming" in segment C. But it is important to note that it is also contrasted sharply on the descending side with D'. There the sign of the Son of Man "appears." Yes, Jesus is leaving the temple here at the beginning of the chiasm. But the chiasm is all about when he will come again. We will see that clearly when we get to the descending side.

A B C D E F G H I J K L M Z M' L' K' J' I' H' G' F' E' D' C' B' A'

Thrown down (24:1b-2)

"[W]hen his disciples came to point out to him the buildings of the temple. But he answered them, 'You see all these, do you not?

---

30   "When the Lord departed from the temple, all the buildings of the Law and the structure of the Commandments were so overthrown." St. Jerome, quoted in Aquinas, *Catena Aurea*, Matthew 24:1-2. "Christ . . . while He was in it, had upheld the temple that it should not fall." Origen, quoted in Aquinas, *Catena Aurea*, Matthew 24:1-2. Also St. Bede, cited in Aquinas, *Catena Aurea*, Mark 13:1-2.

31   St. Ambrose, quoted in Aquinas, *Catena Aurea*, Luke 21:5-8. Origen agreed that "each man, being the temple of God by reason of the Spirit of God dwelling in him, is himself the cause of his being deserted, that Christ should depart from him." Quoted in Aquinas, *Catena Aurea*, Matthew 24:1-2.

Truly, I say to you, there will not be left here one stone
upon another that will not be thrown down.'"

As we approach segment E, the disciples should really amaze us with their out-of-touch comment. Jesus has just spoken woeful judgment on the temple's leadership. We can imagine the disciples standing to one side nodding their heads in approval. Like many common Jews of the day, they had little affection for their leadership. But after this confrontation, the disciples foolishly point out to Jesus the beauty of the temple structure![32]

Perhaps they are expressing the hope that the coming in blessing that Jesus mentioned would happen soon. More likely, they are salivating over the idea of taking control of the temple's administration. If Jesus is leading a New Exodus into the kingdom of God, then the old priesthood and leadership must be eliminated just as it was in the original Exodus. Remember the plagues of Egypt? In the disciples' minds, when Jesus overthrows the old leadership, who will be the beneficiaries? They will! They are probably looking at the temple with the pride and avarice you might see in the eyes of a new car owner. In awe at the temple's glory, they think it will be a magnificent capital for their new kingdom. When, in response to their praise, Jesus declares that the temple *itself* is forsaken, they are aghast.

On one level, this is understandable. The temple complex was a wonder of the ancient world. Set on a hill, from a distance it looked like a great pearl glowing in the sunshine. A pillar of smoke from the sacrifices rose to the heavens: a sign to the Jews that the temple cult connected them to the God

---

32 They said this "because they were foolish and inexperienced." Theophylact of Ohrid, quoted in Aquinas, *Catena Aurea*, Luke 21:5–8.

of heaven. Jews came from all over the world to celebrate the feasts. And the temple hierarchy was at the pinnacle of its influence. Even Rome treated Jerusalem deferentially.

But have the disciples entirely missed the previous "woes"? Have they not seen the sorrow on Jesus' face as he yearned to protect Jerusalem's children? Have they not heard Jesus declare that the temple was "forsaken and desolate"?

Apparently, the disciples have indeed missed all of these things, for they do not yet understand the spiritual nature of Christ's kingdom. So Jesus replies bluntly and unambiguously: The magnificent temple is headed for total destruction. Yes, Jesus will come in blessing someday, but first, desolation will smite the temple into oblivion.

This is the core of the message within the inclusio. Note this, because it is important: The entire chiasm is devoted to the destruction of Jerusalem's temple and its cult within a generation. "All this will come upon this generation."

This idea causes consternation among the disciples. One can imagine Jesus turning to walk to the Mount of Olives and his disciples standing behind him with dropped jaws. How can Jesus be the king of God's kingdom—the royal Son of David—without the temple as his throne room? So they gather themselves, hurrying to follow Jesus for a follow-up question and answer session.

A B C D E F G H I J K L M Z M' L' K' J' I' H' G' F' E' D' C' B' A'

Knowledge sought (24:3a)

"As he sat on the Mount of Olives, the disciples came to him privately, saying, 'Tell us, when will this be?'"

Notice here a telling disconnect between Jesus and his disciples: Jesus has just agonized over the *people* of Jerusalem who are about to be judged, but it is the destruction of the *buildings* of Jerusalem that grabs the attention of the disciples. So the disciples appoint the four most influential among them to question Jesus privately. We learn in Mark 13:3 that it is Peter, James, John, and Andrew who probe Jesus for a clarification. They probably choose their delegation carefully, because they have something very important to ask.

Perhaps their motivation is not immediately obvious. Is it simple curiosity? Or are they looking forward to seeing Jesus recognized as king? Perhaps they are merely attached to the temple and thus concerned for it. Although these are possibilities, I think otherwise. But to discern the reason, we will have to use the knowledge we can garner from Luke 17.

As we will see later, the chiasm here and in Luke 17 points to a motive other than simple curiosity. We won't examine all of the evidence here. Some will emerge in the descending segment F' of this passage; and more in the identical segment that appears in Luke. That evidence will clarify that the disciples want advance knowledge about the events unfolding in Jerusalem for a reason. And in both chiasms Jesus specifically rejects that reason.

Why are they asking? In a nutshell, because knowledge is power. If they are to be leaders in the new kingdom as promised, and if the temple is to be destroyed, then they had better get in front of these events. They need details of the future to be able to plan. With the present temple authorities on the way out, *someone* has to be in control.

Remember, these are the disciples who attempted to keep children away from Jesus because they were not important enough (Mark 10:13; Luke 18:15-16). They had been arguing about personal greatness when they thought Jesus would not notice. These same disciples had approached Jesus shortly before the Olivet Discourse in order to find out which of them would be greatest in his kingdom (Matt. 18:1). Shortly there-after, the brothers James and John had gotten their mother to ask Jesus if he would install them as his two most powerful disciples (Matt. 20:21; Mark 10:42). In a few hours, they will begin to argue over who is greatest—in the *context of the institution of the Eucharist* (Luke 22:24).

These are men who are very interested in personal power. We need not read ill intent into their desire for knowledge. In fact, they will be much different after the descent of the Holy Spirit. But segment F', along with Luke 17, point to a desire for control through knowledge.

At this point in their conversion, they are oblivious to the true role of leadership in the kingdom. In addition, they seem to have no clue about the temple's destruction. Their jumble of questions is evidence of that. They ask Jesus, "When will this be, and what will be the sign of your coming and of the close of the age?"

They ask more than they know. They seem to think that three events—the destruction of the temple, Christ's return in glory, and the end of the age—are all one event.[33] They cannot imagine the end of the temple without the end of the world at the same moment.[34]

We know they are distinct events because we have the advantages of history, Scripture, and the guidance of the Holy Spirit in the authoritative teaching of the Church. In fact, there is not a single Church Father who taught that this

---

33   St. Cyril of Alexandria, "[Christ] forewarned them that . . . the temple . . . would be destroyed. . . . They however understood not the meaning of what was said, but rather imagined that the words He spoke referred to the consummation of the world."Cyril, *A Commentary upon the Gospel of Luke*, trans. R. Payne Smith, (Oxford: University Press, 1859), 139.

34   St. John Chrysostom, "The disciples supposed that Christ's coming should be then, and the end of the world should be when Jerusalem should be destroyed." Quoted in Aquinas, *Catena Aurea*, Matthew 24:3-5.

was merely one question that would have one answer relating to one event.[35]

Note the disciples use three interrogative clauses:[36]

1. "Tell us, when will this be, (the destruction of the temple)?
2. And what will be the sign of your coming (Second Advent)?
3. And of the close of the age" (the final eschaton)?

It seems obvious, from the perspective of history and Church teaching, that the last two clauses are about the same event. Christ will come at the Second Advent—which is also the close of the age (the final eschaton). So, although there are three clauses that can be discussed as three distinct events, it is easier to discuss them as two. We can keep in mind that the second and third events are logically distinct but correspond chronologically.

The structure of the answers that Jesus gives to these questions supports this approach. The inclusio, containing the chiasm within it, marks out the beginning and end of the first answer. Once the inclusio ends, Jesus switches topics to answer the second question. This means there are ultimately two questions contained within these three clauses; and that Jesus answers the two questions one after another.[37]

---

35 Hyperpreterists might be the only group that would claim this is all one event. See Currie, *Rapture*, 465-471, for a discussion of hyperpreterism.

36 Sts. Jerome and Hillary of Poitiers refer to them as three *questions*, which they certainly are. But we are avoiding that language, and using *clauses*, for the sake of clarity when we examine the two answers of Jesus. St. Jerome wrote, "They ask Him three things. First, The time of the destruction of Jerusalem, saying, Tell us when shall these things be? Secondly, The time of Christ's coming, saying, And what shall be the sign of your coming? Thirdly, The time of the consummation of this world, saying, And of the end of the world?" Both quoted in Aquinas, *Catena Aurea*, Matthew 24:3-5.

37 Not long ago most knowledgeable Catholics knew that this passage answered two distinct questions. For example, Cornelius à Lapide's commentary on Matthew handles the passage in this manner, and it was in many pastors' libraries a generation ago.

Indeed, this is the approach of St. John Chrysostom. "When the Lord had finished all that related to Jerusalem, he came in the rest to his own coming."[38] Ambrose, in his commentary on Luke, agreed that the three clauses have only two answers.[39] Finally, considering how St. Thomas laid out his commentary on Matthew, Mark, and Luke—the *Golden Chain*—it appears he was comfortable with two answers to two chronological questions as well.[40]

We find confirming evidence for this streamlined approach in the parallel passages in Mark and Luke. Mark, always one for brevity, condenses Matthew's three clauses into two.[41] These two clauses encompass the same two questions we determined are in Matthew (although Matthew has them in three clauses). Jesus answers them one after the other in Mark just as he does in Matthew.

In Luke 21, the disciples use two interrogative clauses while questioning. From the answer that Jesus gives, we can be sure this is only one chronological question.[42] In that chapter Jesus speaks only of the destruction of the temple. So the idea that more than one clause can be used to ask a single question is evident in Luke as well as in Matthew.

So, we will handle the three clauses as two questions. The

---

38   St. John Chrysostom, quoted in Aquinas, *Catena Aurea*, Matthew 24:23.

39   St. Ambrose pointed out the two clauses (one question) in Luke as being a truncated version of Matthew's three clauses (two questions). "Matthew adds a third question (clause), that both the time of the destruction of the temple, and the sign of His coming, and the end of the world, might be inquired into by the disciples. But our Lord being asked when the destruction of the temple should be, and what the sign of His coming, instructs them as to the signs, but does not mind to inform them as to the time." Quoted in Aquinas, Catena Aurea, Luke 21:5-8.

40   Aquinas, *Catena Aurea*, Matthew 24:3-5.

41   "Tell us, when will this be, and what will be the sign when these things are all to be accomplished?" Mark 13:4. This simplification stands as another evidence of Matthean Priority. Mark is simplifying Matthew's account.

42   "Teacher, when will this be, and what will be the sign when this is about to take place?" Luke 21:7.

first answer is within the aforementioned inclusio, while the second answer follows its end. But St. Augustine raises an important caveat. He understood the second clause in a slightly different manner than we have delineated above. Rather than the "sign of your coming" referring exclusively to the Second Advent, he understood it as referring to the continual coming of Christ to and through his Church. So he understood the second clause as more than just a single event that will occur at the same time as the third clause. The "coming" clause is related to both the first and third clauses but is independent of either in a certain sense. This is an important insight, which we note now and will explore later.

Meanwhile, we can affirm that Augustine saw these three clauses as being answered by two distinct events in time: first the destruction of the temple in A.D. 70 and secondly the final eschaton:

> The Lord gave these replies to the disciples who asked him. . . . We must distinguish through careful consideration which of those signs refers to which. . . . Otherwise we might suppose that what pertains to the destruction of Jerusalem refers to the end of the world. Or just the opposite, we might state that what pertains to the end of the world refers to the destruction of that city.[43]

This is accurate as long as we remember the caveat that the present "comings" of Christ in and through his Church at all times are essential to Augustine's understanding of the passage.

---

43 St. Augustine, *The Works of Saint Augustine*, Epistle 199, 340:25-26. I inserted italic numbers for clarity. I deleted the mention of "comings" between (1) and (2) in the quotation because we will discuss it in detail later.

In summary, Jesus will give two separate answers to these two chronologically distinct questions. There are two different events discussed in two answers, separated by what is already close to 2,000 years and counting. Segment F contains the first of these questions: *When* will the temple be destroyed? This encompasses the answer contained within the inclusio.

The benefit of hindsight

It is easier for us to understand the *when* than it could possibly have been for the disciples. For starters, we can take note of when we are still within the inclusio and when it has ended. The first question of the disciples is about *when* the temple will be destroyed. If we are within the inclusio, that question is still being addressed. Furthermore, we are able to look back at history to fill in the knowledge that they are asking to have ahead of time.

We have already discussed the assault on Jerusalem by Vespasian and his son, Titus. When Jerusalem falls, the human devastation will be enormous. The Romans will overwhelm the temple grounds about a month before they subdue the entire city. In the melee, a fire will break out in the temple buildings. The stones of the temple structure will survive the raging fire, but the gold of the temple will melt and flow between the stones of the building. Titus won't wish to leave it there. So, after Jerusalem is subdued, the Romans will spend three years dismantling the stones to get at that gold.

All that is left of the temple today is the Western Wall— the foundation stones of the outer wall of the complex. Not only the temple, but all "the fortifications they [the Romans] so completely leveled with the ground, that persons who approached would scarcely have believed that the city had ever been inhabited."[44] Titus will leave only three towers of Jerusalem standing as a sign to future generations of what a great city Jerusalem had been before it rebelled against Rome. The stones at which the disciples had marveled will be gone forever.

This is the *when* that we know in hindsight. The disciples, of course, did not have this perspective in A.D. 30. On the descending side of the chiasm, segment F' will highlight the *uncontrollability* of these events. The *when* of Jerusalem's fate was strictly God's purview, not theirs.

A B C D E F **G** H I J K L M Z M' L' K' J' I' H' G' F' E' D' C' B' A'

Signs of coming (24:3b)

"[A]nd what will be the sign of your coming and of the close of the age?"

The second question of the disciples is contained here in segment G. Jesus will not fully answer it until we get past the end of the inclusio, which focuses primarily on the destruction of the temple. Within the inclusio, the only direct answer to this second question is in its descending partner, segment G'. That should not surprise us. As we will discover when we get there, even in that segment it is given primarily for contrast.

This is a good time to sum up Jesus' overall approach in answering these two separate questions. In the first question, the disciples ask for the *when* of the temple's destruction. Jesus proceeds to tell them that his *coming in the judgment of A.D. 70* will be preceded by eight signs, and he delineates these signs within the inclusio. We will discuss them one by one.

---

44   Flavius Josephus, *Wars of the Jews*, 1, 7.

They also asked him about the end of the age in their second question (contained here in segment G). This discussion of his *coming at the end of the world* will be discussed after the inclusio ends. That coming, as we will discover, will be largely without signs.

A B C D E F G H I J K L M Z M' L' K' J' I' H' G' F' E' D' C' B' A'

Sign One: False messiahs (24:4-5)

"And Jesus answered them, 'Take heed that no one leads you astray.
For many will come in my name, saying,
"I am the Christ," and they will lead many astray.'"

What is particularly striking about this answer is its emphasis. The disciples want to know about *when*. They seek signs that will give them control over the future. Jesus does give them signs to forewarn them of the temple's destruction, but that is not his main concern.[45] He shows much more concern about the coming false messiahs, and here he issues an urgent warning not to follow them and be led astray.

Jesus' disciples have just shown themselves to be naive and disconnected from the reality that is about to descend on Jerusalem. Yet, in just a matter of days these men will be the leaders of Christ's fledgling Church. It will do the Church little good to survive Jerusalem's destruction only to lose the truth of the Faith to the false christs who will spring up after the Ascension. These false christs are *sign one*.

Jesus' concern is justified, and this sign came to pass as he predicts. During the period leading up to the Jewish-Roman

---

45   St. John Chrysostom noted this, "His first answer is neither concerning the destruction of Jerusalem, nor concerning His second coming, but concerning the evils which were to be immediately encountered." Quoted in Aquinas, *Catena Aurea*, Matthew 24:3-5.

War in A.D. 67, there appeared several false christs in Judea,[46] and their message was always the same: "Join me and God will empower us to defeat the Romans!"[47] We know the names of the three main leaders of this time: Eleazar, John, and Simon. In fact, by the time Titus hems in Jerusalem with a tight siege, the factions of these three leaders within the city walls are busy fighting not only the Romans but each other.[48] These false messiahs will be hunted down and killed.[49] Their followers will be killed or sold into slavery.

And so Jesus' followers will be witnesses to not one but two wars: the Roman war on Jerusalem and the false messiahs' war on the Church.

The similarity between H and H' in the chiasm demonstrates the importance that Jesus gave to this warning. They are not merely related topics, as some corresponding parts of a chiasm are: They have an identical message. Jesus knows that many Jews will follow these false prophets promising to change the course of history. But he declares that the events about to overtake Jerusalem and her temple are beyond human control. The God of Israel is going to dictate history, and no human leader will be able to change that. Better to step in front of a stampeding herd of horses than to stand between Jerusalem and God's coming judgment.

---

46 "Imposters and deceivers persuaded the multitude to follow them into the wilderness, and pretended that they would exhibit manifest wonders and signs, that should be performed by the providence of God. And many that were prevailed on by them suffered the punishments of their folly." Flavius Josephus, *Antiquities of the Jews, The Life and Works of Flavius Josephus*, trans. William Whiston, (Peabody, MA: Hendrickson, nd), 20, 8:6.

47 "For many came forward, when destruction was hanging over Jerusalem, saying that they were Christs." St. Bede, quoted in Aquinas, *Catena Aurea*, Mark 13:6.

48 "At the time of the Jewish captivity, there were many leaders who declared themselves to be Christs, so that while the Romans were actually besieging them, there were three factions within." St. Jerome, quoted in Aquinas, *Catena Aurea*, Matthew 24:23-28.

49 Tacitus, *The Histories* (109 AD), trans. Alfred John Church and William Jackson Brodribb, (London: Macmillan, 1927), 5. Eleazar was killed first by John's men. Then John and Simon were killed by the Romans.

When there arise men who claim to speak as God's Anointed One in order to muster an army against the Romans, the disciples are to recognize this as *sign one* of the temple's demise. But the destruction is not yet imminent.

A B C D E F G H I J K L M Z M' L' K' J' I' H' G' F' E' D' C' B' A'

Signs Two, Three, Four: Time of suffering protracted (24:6-8)

"And you will hear of wars and rumors of wars; see that you are not alarmed; for this must take place, but the end is not yet. For nation will rise against nation, and kingdom against kingdom, and there will be famines and earthquakes in various places: all this is but the beginning of the birth-pangs."

In segment I, we encounter signs two, three, and four. These are grouped together because they all speak of a lack of stability. Political upheaval will be the norm. Societal conventions will disappear, food supplies will grow scarce, and even terra firma itself will be untrustworthy.

The outbreak of "wars and rumors of wars" throughout the empire is *sign two*. The decade of the sixties was for Rome a more serious version of what the 1960s were for the United States. Society appeared to be disintegrating. The *Pax Romana*, the Roman-imposed peace that reigned throughout the ancient world, had deteriorated. Some political observers of the first century believed that the Roman Empire itself would not survive the turmoil.[50] The decade began with rebellion in Britain and ground on with the Jewish-Roman War in Judea. In between, the unheard-of

---

50   Vespasian "foresaw already the civil wars which were coming upon them, nay, that the very government was in danger." Josephus, *Wars of the Jews*, 5, 8:1.

actually happened: A Caesar committed suicide and civil war erupted within the walls of Rome itself. Three generals fought for the right to be the next Caesar, and by the time Vespasian emerged in A.D. 69, the civil war had touched virtually all of the empire in one way or another.

Amazingly, Jesus assures his disciples that they should not be disturbed by these wars. "See that you are not alarmed; for this must take place, but the end is not yet." Imagine that! The entire civilized world will soon be disintegrating, and Jesus tells his followers not to sweat it.

Why? Simple: The danger to the Church lies not in the wars but in the destruction of Jerusalem. The wars will be only a preliminary warning sign before "the end." The Christians are to be wary of the end of Jerusalem because it had the potential to decapitate the Church. If the Church leadership were to be trapped in the slaughter, it would be devastating.

So the end mentioned here, once again, is not meant to be understood as the end of the world, but rather the end of the temple. This is as we should expect, since we are still within the inclusio. But the disciples, hearing this for the first time, most likely think that the beginning of the wars signals the beginning of the final end.[51]

Famine is *sign three*. And sure enough, as the early Church historian Eusebius of Caesarea documented, in the mid-to-late forties "the world was visited with a famine, which writers that are entire strangers to our religion have recorded in

---

51   St. John Chrysostom believed that Jesus was correcting the false impression of the disciples, who believed that the end of Jerusalem necessitated the end of the world. "Because this might alarm the disciples, He continues, 'See that you be not troubled.' And because they supposed that the end of the world would follow immediately after the war in which Jerusalem should be destroyed, He corrects their suspicions concerning this, 'These things must come to pass, but the end is not yet.'" Quoted in Aquinas, *Catena Aurea,* Matthew 24:6–8.

their histories."[52] The best we can piece together is that the non-Christian Jews of Jerusalem were able to obtain food through the temple administration. Queen Helena of Adiabene and her son Izates were Gentile converts to Judaism. As the famine raged, she purchased food in Egypt and Cyprus to feed the needy in Jerusalem.[53] (The Jews repaid this generous gift when she died, erecting for her a fantastic tomb.[54]) But since the food she donated was probably distributed by the temple authorities, who were suppressing Christianity at the time, likely very little was given to the Christians. St. Paul refers to this famine in 2 Corinthians 8:11-14 and seems to have been regularly collecting donations from the Gentile Christians to ameliorate the suffering of the Church in Judea.

But even this famine was minor in comparison to what descended on Jerusalem during the Roman siege. When the war began, the city had enough food stored to feed itself for twenty-one years.[55] But as the war progressed, the three factions of Jews within Jerusalem burned one another's food stores, greatly worsening the effects of the siege and dooming many innocent Jews of Jerusalem to slow starvation. Josephus described it thusly:

> Of those that perished by famine in the city, the number was prodigious, and the miseries they underwent were unspeakable. . . . The dearest friends fell to fighting one with another . . . snatching from each other the most miserable supports of life. . . . Their hunger was so intol-

52   Eusebius Pamphilius of Caesarea, *Ecclesiastical History*, trans. Kirsopp Lake, (New York: Harvard University Press, 1980), 2:8.

53   Josephus, *Antiquities*, 20:2. Adiabene was in modern day Iraq. The queen is also mentioned in the Talmud.

54   Pausanias singled out her tomb as one of the most wonderful anywhere in the ancient world. Pausanias, *Description of Greece*, trans. W.H. Jones and H.A. Ormerod (Boston: Harvard University Press, 1933), 8, 16:4-5.

55   Josephus, *War of the Jews*, 5, 1:4.

erable, that . . . the very leather which belonged to their shields they pulled off and gnawed.[56]

Sign four involves earthquakes. During this period there were two earthquakes of such destructive force that we still know about them. In the first, the city of Colossae in modern Turkey was totally destroyed about two decades after Jesus spoke these words. (This is one method of dating the Epistle to the Colossians. The Church there did not exist after the earthquake, because the city did not exist.) Pompeii was the site of the other large earthquake—in A.D. 63—just a few years before the Jewish-Roman War began. Less than a decade after the Romans destroyed Jerusalem's temple, Pompeii would be utterly destroyed, buried under volcanic ash.

Amazingly, Jesus says that this would be just "the beginning of the sufferings." Origen likened these three signs to a disease that slowly progresses through a body long before it is fatal: "As the body sickens before the death of the man," so the destruction takes time.[57] Soon, Jesus will point out a sign that would demand immediate action and require faith to endure—but not quite yet.

A B C D E F G H I J K L M Z M' L' K' J' I' H' G' F' E' D' C' B' A'

Tribulation (24:9)

"Then they will deliver you up to tribulation, and put you to death; and you will be hated by all nations for my name's sake."

The theme in J is identical to that in J': the approaching tribulation, commonly called the Great Tribulation. All of a

---

56   Josephus, *Wars of the Jews*, 6, 3:3.
57   Origen, quoted in Aquinas, *Catena Aurea*, Matthew 24:6-8.

sudden, the signs get personal. *Sign five* involves hatred for—
and even the death of—the followers of Jesus. The focus of
this Great Tribulation, as it is for John in Revelation, is not
Jerusalem but the Church.[58]

From the parallel passage in Luke, we can be sure that this
tribulation occurred during the first century. Luke records
that the persecutors "will arrest you and persecute you;
they will hand you over to synagogues and prisons" (21:12).
Mark adds the detail that there will be beatings of Christians in the synagogues (13:9). Have you heard recently of
Christians being arrested on the authority of a synagogue?
Have you noticed any newspaper articles about a good, old-
fashioned flogging of Christians in a synagogue? Of course
you haven't. This is speaking of events that occurred before
the destruction of Jerusalem. The temple authorities were
persecuting the Christians, and their jurisdiction was recognized in the scattered synagogues.

Even in this bad news, however, there is a seed of good.
Jesus predicts that when they are put on trial, the Holy Spirit
will give them the words to say. They, typical common folk,
will be empowered to witness to Jesus in the highest ech-
elons of society (cf. Mark 13:11).

Jesus predicts that this will be the worst tribulation ever,
and he will be proven right. The temple authorities sought
to silence this new sect of Christians almost immediately,
and they were zealous in the task. The apostles were jailed
and beaten. Stephen was stoned to death. The authorities
sent Saul out in search of more Christians to persecute. But
their reach was limited. What transformed this develop-
ing persecution into the Great Tribulation was the use of
Roman authority. At first, the empire kept this squabble

---

58   Currie, *Rapture*, 106-131, 171-175, 243-276; for a detailed discussion of the Great Tribulation.

between two Jewish groups at arm's length. What caused it to decide that the Christians were true enemies of the Roman state?

In July of A.D. 64, almost two-thirds of Rome burned to the ground. It was widely believed that Nero had set the fire in an attempt at urban renewal, so Nero deflected the intense citizen anger by blaming the Christians. Christians were declared politically seditious for their beliefs—enemies of humanity—and Rome started to hunt them down. Suddenly, Christians found themselves "hated by all nations" because of Christ. Gentile governors and kings joined the persecution, as Mark 13:9 and Luke 21:12 had predicted. Many Christians met their death in Rome's Coliseum as audiences jeered. Some were strapped to stakes and burned alive as human torches in Nero's gardens.[59] Both Peter and Paul were martyred in Rome during this time.[60]

Why was this tribulation worse than any other? Simply put, because the Church was so vulnerable. Humanly speaking, the Church was small, poor, and politically weak. It had not penetrated much of the world outside of the empire. Within a few short years, the top echelon of its leadership was virtually wiped out. The biblical canon had not yet been determined. The only—the only—hope of preserving the truth about Christianity was vested in the hearts and minds of a handful of leaders.

Eusebius, along with the early Church writer Tertullian, points to Nero as the first Roman emperor to persecute the Christians as state strategy.[61] Clement of Rome wrote that "the Neronian persecution had been a wholesale onslaught

---

59   Tacitus, *The Annals*, trans. Alfred John Church and William Jackson Brodribb (Charleston, NC: Nabu Press, 2010), 15:44; 1:15.
60   Sts. Peter and Paul were martyred around A.D. 64–65.
61   Eusebius, *Ecclesiastical History*, 11:25.

of reckless fury."[62] Others just as ruthless as Nero would follow him, but the Church's "bench" would have more depth
by then. Never again was the Church as vulnerable as it was
under Nero.

Of course, all these signs may very well also point to
events that will occur before the final end. As we will note
later, nothing would fit the pattern of scriptural prophecy
better. St. Ambrose reminded us that we are always in the
last times, and so "diseases of the world shall go before."[63]
But we must be careful to remember that the primary fulfillment—the Great Tribulation—occurred in the years
leading up to A.D. 70.

A B C D E F G H I J **K** L M Z M' L' K' J' I' H' G' F' E' D' C' B' A'

Sign Six: Do not fall away (24:10-11)

*"And then many will fall away, and betray one another, and hate one
another. And many false prophets will arise and lead many astray."*

Sign six—widespread apostasy—is closely related to the false
messiahs of sign one and the tribulation of sign five. In K,
Jesus predicts a great desertion from the truth. Of course,
there will always be some that "fall away" from the truth;
but when intense tribulation descends on the Church, apostasy will haunt it on a widespread scale.

Did I say earlier that the Church would be witness to two
wars, the Roman war against Jerusalem and the false messiahs' war against the Church? Add a third war: that waged

---

62   Clement of Rome stressed that even the persecution of Domitian did not equal the com-
     prehensive thoroughness of Nero's assault. Clement of Rome (Clement I), *The Apostolic
     Fathers* Volume 1, trans. Kirsopp Lake (Whitefish, MT: Literary Licensing, 2011), 81.
63   St. Ambrose, quoted in *New Catholic Encyclopedia* (New York, McGraw Hill, 1967),
     Apocalypse article.

by the apostates. During the Great Tribulation, as Rome fought to end the Church's very existence, it was abetted by turncoat Christians who hated and betrayed Christ's faithful followers, just as Christ said they would.[64]

The New Testament writers give evidence of the false prophets and apostates who arose almost immediately after the Church began. St. Jerome pointed to Simon of Samaria in Acts. Philip, Peter, and John brought Simon into the Church, but later he apostatized, claiming, "I am the Word of God, I am the Almighty, I am all things of God" (Acts 8). Jerome also pointed to the antichrists mentioned by John, saying, "I suppose all heresiarchs to be Antichrists, and under the name of Christ to teach those things which are contrary to Christ."[65] St. Paul equated the peril caused by false brethren to that of robbers and sea storms.[66]

We learn another difficult truth in the parallel passages in Mark 13 and Luke 21: The "hate" and "betrayal" that tribulation spawns will even tear at family structures. "Brother will deliver up brother to death, and the father his child, and children will rise against parents and have them put to death" (Luke 21:12-13). St. Gregory of Nyssa lived in the fourth century, when such betrayals were still fresh in the memory:[67]

---

64 St. John Chrysostom noted three threats. "Seest thou the war to be threefold? from the deceivers, from the enemies, from the false brethren." John Chrysostom, Homily 75:2, Matthew 24, 2; in Philip Schaff, ed., *Nicene and Post-Nicene Fathers*, volume 10 (Oxford: Parker, 1891).

65 St. Jerome quoted in Aquinas, *Catena Aurea*, Matthew 24:3-5. St. John mentioned antichrists in 1 John 2:18, 22; 4:3; and 2 John 1:7.

66 "Three times I have been shipwrecked; a night and a day I have been adrift at sea; on frequent journeys, in danger from rivers, danger from robbers, danger from my own people, danger from Gentiles, danger in the city, danger in the wilderness, danger at sea, danger from false brethren" 2 Corinthians 11:25-26. Galatians 2:4 makes clear that St. Paul used false brethren as a term for heretics or false prophets.

67 St. Bede claimed that such family betrayals were still remembered in his day. "This has often been seen in time of persecution, nor can there be any firm affection amongst men who differ in faith." Quoted in Aquinas, *Catena Aurea*, Mark 13:9-13.

Let us consider the state of things at that time. While all men were suspected, kinsfolk were divided against one another . . . the gentile son stood up as the betrayer of his believing parents, and of his believing son the unbelieving father became the determined accuser.[68]

Family betrayal strikes much closer to home than being hated by a stranger. This was not lost on the ancients any more than it would be lost on us.

We are the more galled by the persecutions we suffer from those of whose dispositions we made sure, because together with the bodily pain we are tormented by the bitter pangs of lost affection.[69]

This segment speaks of hate and betrayal and falling away. Its corresponding segment K' will speak of fleeing from danger. The first—falling away—is condemned, while Jesus actually urges his followers to flee. It can be a very wise thing to run from danger![70]

A B C D E F G H I J K L M Z M' L' K' J' I' H' G' F' E' D' C' B' A'

Wickedness (24:12)

*"And because wickedness is multiplied,
most men's love will grow cold."*

Here in segment L of the chiasm, Jesus warns that the Great Tribulation will see wickedness increase, dampening Chris-

---

68 St. Gregory of Nyssa, quoted in Aquinas, *Catena Aurea*, Luke 21:1-19.
69 St. Gregory of Nazianzus, quoted in Aquinas, *Catena Aurea*, Luke 21:1-19.
70 St. Paul urged his disciples to flee lust and idolatry. 1 Corinthians 6:18, 10:14; 1 Timothy 6:11; 2 Timothy 2:22.

tian ardor. Although this is certainly not meant to be taken as a good thing, Jesus' words contain a kernel of hope. As Jerome reminded us, "Observe, [it is] the love of many [that will grow cold], not 'of all.' For in the Apostles, and those like them, love would continue."[71] The apostles kept their love "red-hot," while the love of the "many grew cold." So even in this bleak prediction, Paul's hopeful cry can be heard: "Who shall separate us from the love of Christ?" Nothing, if we hold fast to Christ—not even tribulation and persecution.[72]

Externals cannot separate a Christian from God's love. But, as Jesus predicts here, wickedness can. The antipathy between right love and wrong living has been long expounded by the Church. Sin drives love from the soul, the love grows cold, and the supernatural life within dies. Love and iniquity will not coexist. "In proportion as each surrenders himself to iniquity, in that proportion will the flame of love in his heart be extinguished."[73]

In all of Scripture, Nicolaus is perhaps the best example of this.[74] He began well. He was a Gentile proselyte to Judaism who converted to Christianity so early that he became one of the first seven deacons appointed by the apostles (Acts 6:5). He started out in the company of superstars like Stephen, the very first Christian martyr. But by the time of

71 St. Jerome, cited in *Catena Aurea,* on Matthew 24:9-14.
72 "Who shall separate us from the love of Christ? Shall *tribulation, or distress, or persecution,* or famine, or nakedness, or peril, or sword? As it is written, "For thy sake we are being killed all the day long; we are regarded as sheep to be slaughtered." No, in all these things we are more than conquerors through him who loved us. For I am sure that neither death, nor life, nor angels, nor principalities, nor things present, nor things to come, nor powers, nor height, nor depth, nor anything else in all creation, will be able to separate us from the love of God in Christ Jesus our Lord." Romans 8:35-39.
73 Remigius of Auxerre, quoted in Aquinas, *Catena Aurea,* Matthew 24:9-14.
74 St. Hilary of Poitiers made this connection in his Commentary on St. Matthew's Gospel, one of the oldest extant commentaries on Matthew. "Such was Nicolaus, one of the seven deacons, who led astray many by his presences." Quoted in Aquinas, *Catena Aurea,* Matthew 24:9-14.

the Great Tribulation, the heresy of the Nicolaitans bore his name.[75] What was their distinguishing feature? In theory, they held to a form of Gnosticism that taught that once one accepted the truth of Christianity, one was free to live as he desired. In practice, they held to a doctrine of promiscuity. They soon died out as a Christian community because, as this segment makes clear, wickedness and love of God do not coexist. One will triumph over the other.

We sometimes think that we live in a wicked time of history. I tend to agree. You may remember the mantra of the 1960s: "If it feels good, do it." Popular culture in the West has done little more than regress since then. But that idea is nothing more than a rehash of the Nicolaitan dogma. Our age is not the first, nor will it be the last, in which the few will strive to keep their love "red-hot" in the face of wickedness. "Most men's love" will "grow cold" when wickedness multiplies. Indeed, wickedness always comes this way, so we must always be on guard against its allure.

A B C D E F G H I J K L **M** Z M' L' K' J' I' H' G' F' E' D' C' B' A'

The end (24:13)

"But he who endures to the end will be saved."

As we approach the climax of the chiasm, Jesus inserts a word of hope. All is not lost.[76] Indeed, segments M and M' form a sandwich of good news around the climax. The disciples

---

75   There is some debate on his culpability, but the lessons stand regardless and are mentioned in Revelation 2:6-15. They are also mentioned in Irenaeus, *Against Heresies*, 3, 11:1; and in the writings of Hippolytus, *The Refutation of all Heresies*, 7, 24; both in Alexander Roberts, with James Donaldson and A. Cleveland Coxe, ed. *Ante-Nicene Fathers: The Writings of the Fathers Down to A.D. 325* (Edinburgh: T&T Clark, 1870).

76   This is always the case, according to St. Paul. "We know that in everything God works for good with those who love him, who are called according to his purpose" (Rom. 8:28).

are promised that if a person faithfully endures to the end of
the Great Tribulation, he will be saved. In this, Jesus is surely
referring to eternal salvation, since he has already predicted
that one consequence of the tribulation for his followers will
be bodily death. But Jesus assures them that death will not be
their *ultimate* destiny. He will conquer death, so he will meet
them again on the other side, in the life after death.

The salvation promised, however, requires endurance.
Gregory of Nyssa expressed beautifully the role of patient
endurance in our salvation.

> [Through the practice of patient endurance] we begin to
> possess that very thing which we are. . . . The posses-
> sion of the soul is laid in the virtue of patience, because
> patience is the root and guardian of all virtues. Now pa-
> tience is to endure calmly the evils which are inflicted by
> others, and also to have no feeling of indignation against
> him who inflicts them.[77]

This call to endurance is not unique to the Christians who
will suffer in the Great Tribulation. When Christ sends his
disciples to preach to "the lost sheep of the house of Israel,"
he makes this same promise that "he who endures to the end
will be saved" (Matt. 10:5-22). Do not forget that Judas Iscariot
was one of the Twelve who heard that admonition. He did not
avoid the wickedness that caused his love to grow cold, and he
fell miserably. To hear the promise is not to attain the end.

Judas was given great access to truth and grace. From
those to whom much is given, much is required. The Christian given more truth will also be buffeted more severely to

---

77   It's that last phrase that is so tough in practice. St. Gregory of Nyssa, quoted in Aquinas,
      Catena Aurea, Luke 21:1-19.

test his faith. As Origen put it, "Morally; he who shall see that glorious second coming of the word of God into his soul, must needs suffer in proportion to the measure of his proficiency, assaults of opposing influences."[78]

In the Olivet Discourse, the disciples—and we as well—are given much. We must endure to the end to win the prize of salvation.

A B C D E F G H I J K L M Z M' L' K' J' I' H' G' F' E' D' C' B' A'

Preach the gospel of the kingdom (24:14)

"And this gospel of the kingdom will be preached throughout the whole world, as a testimony to all nations; and then the end will come."

This brings us to the climax of the chiasm, and to *sign seven:* evangelization. This sign is the only one that lies within the power of the disciples. Jesus clearly tells his disciples that the end of the temple will not occur before the gospel is "preached throughout the whole world." Not until the gospel has been fully proclaimed will the old religious order be destroyed.

As we have observed, the inclusio and the chiastic structure of this discourse assure us that all of these verses refer to the *end of the second temple* in A.D. 70. And yet, sign seven seems to negate that idea. After all, although the apostles brought the gospel as far as India, could they have reached the Far East? We can be quite confident that the disciples did not travel to the Americas, nor to the Australian continent. So, perhaps this sign did *not* get fulfilled before the end of the temple.

But to say this would be to place too much emphasis on the English translation and ignore the Greek terminology

---

78   Origen, quoted in Aquinas, *Catena Aurea*, Matthew 24:9-14.

used in Matthew. The Greek word for *world* in this passage is *oikoumene*, which specifically designates the civilized world, delineated at the time by the boundaries of the Roman Empire. There is another word for *world* that denotes the entire earth: *kosmos*.[79] But that is not used here. Jesus is predicting that before the end comes to the temple the gospel must be preached throughout the entire known, civilized world: the Roman Empire.

Even though he died in the Great Tribulation, Paul wrote under divine inspiration that this sign had been fulfilled. He used the same word as Jesus, *oikoumene*, to claim that in his lifetime the Faith "is proclaimed in all the world" (Rom. 1:8).

The early Church agreed. St. Clement of Rome—bishop during the Jewish-Roman War—wrote that Peter and Paul had been martyred, but not before they had "taught righteousness to the whole world."[80] So, one of the very first popes evidently believed the seventh sign was fulfilled prior to the fall of Jerusalem.[81]

Eusebius explicitly made the connection: First the gospel was preached, and only then did destruction descend on Jerusalem. "The teaching of the New Covenant was borne to all nations, and at once the Romans besieged Jerusalem and destroyed it and the temple."[82] He made clear that the apostles had fanned out throughout the civilized world to fulfill this prediction of Jesus.[83]

---

79 This word for *world* is used in Matthew 24:21. So Matthew was using both words.
80 Clement of Rome was Pope from 67-73 AD. Clement, *First Epistle of Clement to the Corinthians*, 5; in Roberts, *Ante-Nicene Fathers*.
81 Justin Martyr also wrote that "from Jerusalem there went out into the world, men, twelve in number, and . . . by the power of God they proclaimed to every race of men that they were sent by Christ to teach to all the word of God." Justin Martyr, *The First Apology*, 39, in Roberts, *Ante-Nicene Fathers*.
82 Eusebius Pamphilius of Caesaria, *Demonstratio Evangelia: The Proof of the Gospel*, trans. W.J. Ferrar (New York, Macmillan Company, 1920), 1:6.
83 Eusebius, *Ecclesiastical History*, 3:1.

St. John Chrysostom declared this accomplishment to be "the strongest proof of Christ's power, that in thirty years or a little more, the word of the gospel filled the ends of the world."[84]

This was not an easy task. Every one of the apostles, save John, died a martyr's death. Jesus' gospel was resisted by those who believed in the "gospel of Augustus"—Caesar Augustus. When he took the throne of Rome, Augustus declared himself a "savior" who had been sent by "Providence." Rome solemnly promulgated that none before and none to come would ever surpass the glad tidings—the "gospel"—of Augustus' ascension to the throne.[85]

So when the apostles preached the gospel of God's kingdom, they were directly contradicting the secular utopian gospel of the Roman Empire. Rome had declared that its government, with its plans and programs, was all that any reasonable person could possibly need or had the right to expect. Rome would provide civil peace and a chance for prosperity—so don't rock the boat. Does this sound vaguely familiar to the modern ear?

Along came the apostles: few in number, devoid of secular authority, and not well placed on the societal pecking order. They came with the message that Roman utopian answers were not enough. Christ could change your heart, fill it with God's supernatural love, imbue you with hope—but

---

84   St. John Chrysostom "After the gospel is preached in every part of the world, Jerusalem is destroyed . . . which also is a very great sign of Christ's power . . ." John Chrysostom, *Homily 75*, Matthew 24, 2.

85   From an inscription dated to just before the birth of Jesus in Priene (Turkey) commemorating Emperor Augustus' new Roman calendar: "Providence . . . [has sent] us and our descendants a savior, who has put an end to war and established all things... And since the Caesar through his appearance has exceeded the hopes of all former glad tidings, surpassing not only the benefactors who came before him but also leaving no hope that anyone in the future would surpass him, and since for the world the birthday of the god was the beginning of his glad tidings [gospel] . . . .. "PBS," http://www.pbs.org/wgbh/pages/frontline/shows/religion/maps/arch/recovering.html.

only if you believed and repented from your wicked, selfish ways. Salvation was not a corporate affair; it was a personal rebirth that would then transform society. Belief and baptism would bring you citizenship in God's kingdom, which, unlike Rome, would last forever!

Two millennia later, few ever think of Augustus or his utopian claims. Yet many speak to and about Jesus Christ every day. After these many centuries we still proclaim the gospel of the kingdom that the apostles preached throughout the Roman Empire before Jerusalem was destroyed. The King has come and wants to adopt you as his royal child for all eternity. Becoming part of his family will be your salvation from the obliteration of death. You need not view death as an end. This was the message that turned the empire upside-down. This is still the message that can turn the present world aright again.

And so, the central message of this discourse, its climax, dovetails with the coming Great Commission in Matthew 28:19. Since that has not been rescinded, since it is still our duty to preach the gospel to the whole world, this passage stands as a challenge to us in our own day. Indeed, the Church takes this climax and applies it to our present situation, even though the end of Jerusalem is the focus of this segment.[86] Evangelization of the known world remains our task as we await the Second Coming.

Descent down the chiasm

As we begin down the other side of the chiasm, let us regroup. The last segment represented not only the top of the chiasm but also the climax of Jesus' answer. The disciples ask when the temple will be destroyed. Jesus replies by giving them eight

---

86   We will return to this teaching of the Church shortly.

signposts. In the ascending portion of the chiasm, we discovered six of the eight. The climax contained the seventh sign. They ask for a calendar, but Christ gives them a charge and a chore.

The first four signs are an early warning system: The false prophets, the wars, the famines, and the earthquakes tell Jesus' followers that the end is approaching but not yet imminent. The next three signs are more immediate and personal. There will be the Great Tribulation and the apostasy of many Christians. The seventh and climactic sign is also a task to accomplish: evangelizing the Roman Empire.

A B C D E F G H I J K L M Z M' L' K' J' I' H' G' F' E' D' C' B' A'

The end (24:14b)

"[A]nd then the end will come."

Have you noticed how intense experiences can skew our perception of time and reality? Pleasure can "make time stand still," while discomfort can make each moment drag on interminably. The latter was true for the Christians during the Great Tribulation under Nero. Segment M' reminds the disciples that even though they may contemplate the fate of endless suffering, there will indeed be an end. God is loving and merciful. Suffering does not go on forever.

Moreover, as segment M told us, Christians who endure to the end will meet salvation on the other side of suffering. This recalls the words of Paul: "We suffer with him in order that we may also be glorified with him" (Rom. 8:17).

This can be difficult to remember during hard times. The mind can "freeze up" if the trial is long and hard enough. All the more reason to remind ourselves: God is a merciful God, and reward follows trial.

A B C D E F G H I J K L M Z M' L' K' J' I' H' G' F' E' D' C' B' A'

Sacrilege (24:15)

"So when you see the desolating sacrilege spoken of by the prophet Daniel, standing in the holy place (let the reader understand) . . ."

The final sign—*sign eight*—appears in this segment. It corresponds to L, which pointed to the multiplication of wickedness. Here L' speaks of unspeakable wickedness, "the desolating sacrilege." The language of "the desolating sacrilege" is borrowed from multiple instances in Daniel.

Historically, sign eight followed on the heels of the previous sign, the proclamation of the gospel throughout the Roman Empire. Paul claimed twice that sign seven had been accomplished before he died, most likely in A.D. 64 or 65. Sign eight burst forth upon the land of Judea shortly thereafter, in 66.

Sign eight was the only sign that required immediate obedience in order to preserve the infant Church in Jerusalem. Any delay would mean the destruction of the Church, so this sign had to be unambiguous. The eighth sign—the desolating sacrilege of Daniel in the holy place—had to be both public and obvious.

Matthew and Mark add a phrase that Jesus did not speak: "Let the reader understand." Both writers evidently believed that this "desolating sacrilege" would be so obvious that the average Jewish Christian reading this in the first century would immediately recognize it for what it was.[87]

The parallel passage in Luke fills in the details about the "desolating sacrilege" so that later generations, even two millennia later, can still recognize it: "When you see Jerusa-

---

87 Another alternative is that Jesus *did* say these words as a challenge to read Daniel's prophecy with more insight. Mark 13:14.

lem surrounded by armies, then know that its desolation has
come near" (21:20). Luke wanted to make sure we connect
Daniel's prophecy to the events of his generation. The early
Church did not miss it. Augustine wrote,

> The abomination of desolation, which was predicted by
> Daniel, came about when Jerusalem was stormed. . . . It is
> clear, therefore, that the abomination of desolation . . . was
> at that time established there.[88]

St. John Chrysostom, likewise, preached that the abomination
of desolation referred to the armies that attacked Jerusalem."[89]

Students of history understand the utter desolation that for-
eign armies leave in their wake. Not all invading armies, however, commit sacrilege. To the Jews, the mere presence of a
Gentile army in Judea would be considered a grave affront to
the holy places. What's more, the Romans marched under the
ensign of a scavenger: the ceremonially "unclean" eagle. Jews
knew that the Roman legions would worship that graven image of an eagle wherever they marched while invading the Jews'
holy land. If the Romans defeated Jerusalem, the Gentile soldiers
would worship that graven image within the temple itself![90]

These words of Jesus contradict the settled opinion of
the Jewish authorities of his day. They taught that Daniel's
desolating sacrilege had come and gone two centuries before—in 168 B.C., when Antiochus Epiphanies had sacri-

---

88   Augustine, *The Works of Saint Augustine*, Epistle 199, 341:28.

89   John Chrysostom, on Matthew 24, 1; in Schaff, *Nicene and Post-Nicene Fathers*. Theophy-
     lact of Ohrid agreed, "He means by 'the abomination of desolation' the entrance of en-
     emies into the city by violence." Theophylact, in Aquinas, *Catena Aurea*, Mark 13:14-20.

90   Roman soldiers did exactly that when the temple fell in 70 AD. "The Romans, upon
     the burning of the holy house itself . . . brought their ensigns to the temple and set them
     over against its eastern gate; and there did they offer sacrifices to them." Josephus, *Wars
     of the Jews*, 6, 6:1.

WHEN WILL THIS BE

ficed swine on the altar of the temple.[91] By this optimistic rabbinic view, all the bad days for the temple are in the past and God's future plan promises only blessings. This will also be the message of the false prophets against whom Jesus is warning his disciples. But Jesus asserts that the power of positive thinking is not going to control Jerusalem's destiny. God's judgment will not be averted.

In Luke, Jesus ties this coming judgment to the entire corpus of the Old Testament prophets—"a fulfillment of all that is written" (21:22). He is not predicting anything novel, but he *is* correcting the prevailing rabbinic interpretation of the Old Testament.

A B C D E F G H I J K L M Z M' L' **K'** J' I' H' G' F' E' D' C' B' A'

Do flee! (24:16–20)

"[T]hen let those who are in Judea flee to the mountains; let him who is on the housetop not go down to take what is in his house; and let him who is in the field not turn back to take his mantle. And alas for those who are with child and for those who give suck in those days! Pray that your flight may not be in winter or on a sabbath."

We saw in segment K that the response of "many" will be to "fall away." But the faithful few, those who are attentive to the eighth and final sign in L', have their orders here in K': Their response must be to flee. In other words, never fall away (K), but be ready to run (K').

We moderns may not immediately notice this, but to any ancient person this command would be entirely counterintuitive. When being invaded, the sensible instinct would have

---

91   This is described in I Maccabees 1:54. Unfortunately, some modern exegetes of Daniel follow the lead of first-century Judaism rather than the three Gospel writers.

been to run *into* the fortified cities for protection—not *out* of them into the open, defenseless country. This was especially true in the case of Jerusalem, a fortress city that was virtually impregnable in its day. It was surrounded by not one, not two, but three strong walls. Its residents had an ample source of fresh water inside the city and had been hoarding food within its granaries for years.[92] As we noted, there was enough food stored within the city to withstand a siege for twenty-one years. No enemy would have had the will to lay siege to any city for that long. And no one in his right mind would flee such a city to take his chances on a cross-country trek through territory patrolled by enemy troops.

Yet that is exactly what Jesus commands. Without delay—without question—without second thought—his followers are to flee Jerusalem when they see the Roman army surrounding the city.

Perhaps even more amazingly, that is precisely what the Christians did. Long before it could be evident that they were doing the prudent thing, most of them escaped to Pella in Transjordan, where they lived under the protection of King Agrippa. Other Jewish Christians escaped to Alexandria in Egypt, and some to Asia Minor. The Christians even brought with them the episcopal chair of St. James, first bishop of Jerusalem.[93] They might be forced to leave their personal belongings behind, but they risked their lives to bring out that symbol of the Church's authority. According

---

92   Tacitus wrote, "Two hills of great height were fenced in by walls which had been skillfully obliqued or bent inwards, in such a manner that the flank of an assailant was exposed to missiles. The rock terminated in a precipice; the towers were raised to a height of sixty feet, where the hill lent its aid to the fortifications, where the ground fell, to a height of one hundred and twenty. . . . Within were other walls surrounding the palace, and, rising to a conspicuous height, the tower Antonia. . . . The temple resembled a citadel, and had its own walls, which were more laboriously constructed than the others." Tacitus, *The Histories*, 5.

93   Eusebius, *Ecclesiastical History*, 7:14.

to Eusebius, as a result of their obedience to Christ's warning through their bishop, no Christians were caught in the
death trap in Jerusalem.[94]

What happened to Jerusalem after the Christians escaped? Vespasian and Titus waged a patient war of isolation, subduing the entire land of Judea before attempting
to conquer Jerusalem. When the three competing groups of
Jews within the city burned each other's food supplies, the
Romans starved the Jews into weakness and then attacked.
They took the temple and then spent a month engaged in
urban warfare within the city.

In the midst of all this, when could the Christians escape
to safety—even those who promptly obeyed Jesus' command to flee? We cannot know for certain, but there seem
to have been two possibilities. Josephus wrote that many
Jews fled Jerusalem immediately after the defeat of General Cestius. As the Jewish army attacked the retreating Romans, the Christians would have been able to escape along
with the Jewish soldiers chasing the Romans. They would
have had to leave immediately—almost in the midst of battle—during the initial confusion. After the initial rush of
Jewish fighters pursuing the Romans out of Jerusalem, the
gates of the city were locked to prevent any entry or exit.
This would have been in A.D. 66.

Eusebius, on the other hand, seems to place the flight in
June of A.D. 68. After Nero's suicide, Vespasian pulled all
of his troops away from the siege of Jerusalem to use them

---

94 "The whole body, however, of the church at Jerusalem, having been commanded by
a divine revelation, entrusted to men of approved piety there before the war, removed
from the city, and dwelt at a certain town beyond the Jordan, called Pella. . . . And when
those that believed in Christ had come thither from Jerusalem . . . the judgment of God
at length overtook . . . and totally destroyed that generation of impious men." Eusebius,
Ecclesiastical History, 3:5 and 5:86. Also Bede, in Aquinas, *Catena Aurea*, Luke 21:20-24.

in Rome. But the general had second thoughts and decided to send back just enough troops to keep Jerusalem under siege but not enough to actually make progress. As the army shuttled back and forth, this opened up a very small window of escape out of the city. Once again, the Christian response needed to have been immediate.

Although we cannot be sure, I believe it was in A.D. 66 that the Christians fled. The horror of Cestius fighting at the very gates of the holy temple fits Daniel's abomination of desolation precisely. Either scenario, however, would have offered a small window of time in which to escape. Moreover, in both cases the Romans were retreating. This would have made it seem almost foolish for the Christians to even attempt to leave Jerusalem, to which God was evidently providing protection. But the leadership of the Church in Jerusalem remembered Christ's words.[95] Without any thought for earthly possessions or human wisdom, they promptly led the Church out and fled for their lives.

Jesus' warning makes it obvious that his command to flee applied to the first century and not to the end of the world.[96] If Jesus had been warning about the end of the world, it would certainly have done no good to flee to the mountains. At the end of the world, those in the mountains will also meet judgment.[97]

---

95   St. Athanasius described the flight of the Jerusalem Church: "Knowing these things [the warning in the Olivet Discourse], the Saints regulated their conduct accordingly." Athanasius, *Apologia de Fuga: Defense of His Flight*, 11; in Schaff, *Nicene and Post-Nicene Fathers*.

96   St. Bede wrote, "It is on record that this was literally fulfilled, when on the approach of the war with Rome and the extermination of the Jewish people, all the Christians who were in that province, warned by the prophecy, fled far away, as Church history relates." Bede in Aquinas, *Catena Aurea*, Mark 13:3-20.

97   There will be a time of no escape at the end of the world. "The *day of the Lord* will come like a thief in the night. When people say, 'There is peace and security,' then sudden destruction will come upon them as travail comes upon a woman with child, and there will be no escape"(1 Thessalonians 5:2-3).

The mention of pregnant women is another clue that this warning is not about the end of the world.[98] For pregnant women, the rigors of travel through the wilderness would have been a great concern in the ancient world—less so today, and certainly not at all at the final eschaton.[99] The mention of the Sabbath is another confirmation. Why worry about an escape on the Sabbath these days? But it made perfect sense in first-century Jerusalem: The city gates were locked every Sabbath. The Christians could not escape from Jerusalem on a Sabbath because no one was allowed to enter or leave on the Jewish day of rest.

A B C D E F G H I J K L M Z M' L' K' **J'** I' H' G' F' E' D' C' B' A'
Tribulation (24:21)
"For then there will be great tribulation, such as has not been from the beginning of the world until now, no, and never will be."

The eight signs have each been described, and now the chiasm continues its descent with a review of the themes covered on the ascending side. The exact precision of these short statements on the descending side of the chiasm serves as evidence that this chiastic structure was consciously formulated.

Segment J' reminds the disciples that the tribulation to come upon them will be unprecedented in its fury, and the statement makes it quite clear that this is not to be the tribulation at the end of the world. It assumes that there have been other tribulations before it, and that there will be more tribulations *after* it.

---

98 St. Augustine wrote, "'Woe to them that are with child,'... made plain what might otherwise have been doubtful, namely, that what was said of the abomination of desolation belonged not to the end of the world, but the taking of Jerusalem." Augustine in Aquinas, *Catena Aurea*, Luke 21:20-24.

99 This was perfectly clear to St. Bede, living in the preindustrial age. "(Those) overladen with the burden of children, (are) in no small measure impede[d in] their forced flight." Bede in Aquinas, *Catena Aurea*, Mark 13:3-20.

It will not be the last tribulation of the Church—there will be many more—but it will be the worst one.

Looking at this same scene in Luke, we can notice Jesus' eternal perspective when he predicts that "not a hair of your head will perish." To the uninitiated, this might sound like a promise that there will be no suffering. But the intended meaning becomes clear in the next phrase, "by your endurance you will gain your souls" (21:18-19). In other words, Christians will certainly die in this tribulation, but they can count on their eternal welfare if they remain faithful.[100]

The early Christians were keenly aware that they could lose their earthly life in the Great Tribulation, but they were unwilling to forfeit their eternal welfare. Paul picked up on this concept—and has been roundly criticized in the modern pulpit for it. Writing to the Corinthian church, he advised that trouble was just around the corner and so they would do well to stay unmarried.

> In view of the *impending crisis*, it is well for you to remain as you are. . . . Do not seek a wife. . . . Those who marry will experience distress in this life, and I would spare you that. I mean, brothers and sisters, the appointed time has grown short; from now on, let even those who have wives be as though they had none. . . . For the *present form* of this world is passing away. I want you to be free from anxieties. The unmarried man is anxious about the affairs of the Lord, how to please the Lord; but the married man is anxious about the affairs of the world, how to please his wife, and his interests are divided (1 Cor. 7:26-34).

---

100 St. Augustine understood this to mean that we will rise again in our own bodies. See Augustine, *The City of God*, trans., Marcus Dods (New York: The Modern Library, 1950), 19.

Now that we have examined Jesus' warnings, Paul makes perfect sense. He was *not* predicting the end of the world within a few short years. His term for the Great Tribulation was "the impending crisis," and he was warning the Corinthians that the peace and tranquility of their lives was about to be destroyed. Neither was he enunciating a rule against marriage for all time until the final eschaton. Rather, Paul saw the eight signs being fulfilled around him and gave practical counsel. When Nero turned his wrath upon the Church, as Jesus had predicted in sign five, Paul knew it would go easier for those with less earthly responsibility. He was helping his flock prepare to "endure to the end" so that they would gain their salvation.

A B C D E F G H I J K L M Z M' L' K' J' I' H' G' F' E' D' C' B' A'

Time of suffering shortened (24:22)

"And if those days had not been shortened, no human being would be saved; but for the sake of the elect those days will be shortened."

After mention of the worst-ever tribulation, segment I' extends a ray of hope. Its parallel, segment I, had declared that the culmination of these events would be slow. There would be birth pangs stretching over years of upheaval leading up to the Great Tribulation. Segment I' promises that once it does finally arrive, the Great Tribulation will be short in duration.[101]

This shortening reminds the disciples of the loving care of their Father. In fact, Mark tells us that it is God who shortens the tribulation (13:20). Horrible suffering is about to

---

101 St. Bede wrote, "The only refuge in such evils is, that God who gives strength to suffer, should abridge the power of inflicting." *Catena Aurea*, Mark 13:3-20.

descend on the Church, but the Lord will make the time of testing shorter than it might otherwise have been, in order to preserve at least a remnant of the elect from perishing.[102]

"Shortening" does not mean that the days were less than twenty-four hours long. Rather, it relates to the typical period of time for testing and purgation in the Old Testament, in which judgment generally extended for three and a half years. For example, when Elijah declared judgment on Israel, God withheld rain for three and a half years (1 Kings 17:1, 18:1). Daniel predicted that the "little horn" (Nero) would make war against Judaism for three and a half years.[103] Centuries later, the Jewish–Roman War extended for . . . precisely three and a half years. It began in February of A.D. 67, and the temple fell in August of A.D. 70.

So, the early Church might have expected the Great Tribulation to last for that same period of time. But, although it was incredibly intense, Nero's persecution of the Christian Church did not last even three years. It began shortly after the burning of Rome in July of A.D. 64, and it appeared that Nero's intention was to continue the persecution until all Christians were wiped from the face of the earth. But when Jerusalem revolted in the summer of A.D. 66, Nero suddenly had a bigger problem on his hands than finding and tor-

---

102 Keep in mind that the shortened time refers to the war on the Church, not the war against Jerusalem.

103 Judaism is described in Daniel using the phrase "the times and the law." These were the two essential elements of Judaism: the Mosaic Law and the Sabbath/feast cycles. Note that in Daniel 7:21-25, it does not specify the length of the war on the saints. The battle with the saints (the Church) is not the same as the battle against the times and law (the temple system). "He shall speak words against the Most High, and shall wear out the saints of the Most High, and shall think to change the times and the law; and they shall be given into his hand for a time, two times, and half a time." Daniel allows in verse 21 that the war on the saints be cut short. "As I looked, this horn made war with the saints, and prevailed over them, until the Ancient of Days came, and judgment was given." See Currie, *Rapture*, 91-105, 254-261, 286-300; for an extensive treatment of Daniel's view of Nero and the war.

menting the peace-loving, productive Christians—he had a full-fledged war with a powerful and rebellious city. The beginning of the Jewish–Roman War effectively suspended Nero's persecution. God used the arrogance of Jerusalem to fulfill Christ's promise to his Church.[104]

Luke expands on this message of hope. When the judgment on Jerusalem begins to unfold, the Christians are to "stand up and raise your heads, because your redemption is drawing near" (21:28). The attention of their persecutors in Rome will be diverted from the fabricated Christian threat to the actual Jerusalem threat. War with Jerusalem will mean relief from the Great Tribulation.

When things are at their worst, when others are "fainting with fear and with foreboding of what is coming on the world," (Luke 21:26), is the moment when Christians shine. We know that the dawn requires the night, that "what is to give light must endure burning,"[105] that the reward requires the trial, that the Resurrection requires the Passion. So we have hope. After Gregory of Nyssa described all the horrors that plagued the fledgling Church, he pointed to these words. He pointed to Christ, who always "turns His words to the consolation of the elect."[106] Ultimately, regardless of what happens to us, we have a "perfect liberty of body and soul. For as the first coming of our Lord was for the restoration of our souls, so will the second be manifested unto the restoration of our bodies."[107] We believe in the eternal justice that will come with the resurrection of the body, and the life everlasting.[108]

---

104 St. Augustine, "Shortening of the days should be understood in this way . . . because they were reduced in number." Augustine, *The Works of Saint Augustine*, Epistle 199, 341:29.

105 This is widely attributed to Viktor Emil Frankl, *Man's Search for Meaning* (Boston: Beacon Press, 1959).

106 St. Gregory of Nyssa in Aquinas, *Catena Aurea*, Luke 21:28-33.

107 Theophylact of Ohrid in Aquinas, *Catena Aurea*, Luke 21:28-33.

108 Of course, the Church teaches we must also strive for justice here on earth in the meantime.

A B C D E F G H I J K L M Z M'L'K'J'I'**H'** G' F' E' D' C' B' A'

False messiahs (24:23-26)

"Then if any one says to you, 'Lo, here is the Christ!' or 'there
he is!' do not believe it. For false Christs and false prophets will
arise and show great signs and wonders, so as to lead astray, if
possible, even the elect. Lo, I have told you beforehand. So, if they
say to you, 'Lo, he is in the wilderness,' do not go out; if they say,
'Lo, he is in the inner rooms,' do not believe it."

Here, Jesus returns to a major concern: the coming false
prophets. If the Church is to survive, Christians must resist
the temptation to join the temporal resistance of the false
messiahs. Jesus introduced the false prophets in H. He mentions them again here in H' to underscore the vital importance of not following them. They will promise that God
can preserve Jerusalem if you join them, but it is a false
promise. Jerusalem cannot be saved.

The early Fathers warned us that false teachers will always attack the Church, so we must hold fast to the truth the
Church preserves and declares.[109] Jesus has just spoken of ex-
ternal trials to his Church, but the antichrists who will seek
to undermine Christian faith from within are perhaps even
more dangerous. Both these threats to the Church have the
same diabolical source, as St. Ambrose knew well:

> Now mystically, the . . . antichrist . . . pollutes the in-
> nermost recesses of the heart . . . because he desires to
> impress firmly on the affections the footstep of his unbe-
> lief. . . . The Devil (using a false teacher) is (still) trying to

---

109 St. Cyril warned that "there shall come some to whom we must not give place." Quoted in Aquinas, *Catena Aurea*, Luke 21:5-8.

besiege "Jerusalem," i.e., any peaceful soul. . . . But when upon any one in trouble the spiritual presence of Christ has shone, the unjust one is cast out, and righteousness begins her reign.[110]

A B C D E F G H I J K L M Z M' L' K' J' I' H' **G'** F' E' D' C' B' A'

Lightning sign (24:27)

"For as the lightning comes from the east and shines as far as the west, so will be the coming of the Son of man."

In G', Jesus emphasizes his point with a contrast. His Second Advent will be dramatically different than anything the false teachers can conjure up. No one will have any doubt when he really does return for the final eschaton and salvation of the world.[111]

This is the only time within the inclusio that Christ's Second Coming is described, yet it is not out of place. First, it stands as the natural complement to segment G. That is the ascending segment in which the disciples ask the second question, about the final eschaton. Secondly, its purpose here is abundantly clear: contrast. Yes, Jesus will come again. But it will not be anything like the announced fanfare that will accompany the arrival of the false messiahs.

The contrast between the false messiahs and Jesus' Second Advent will indeed be stark. The false teachers will work to drum up support, assembling small bands of followers in an

---

110 St. Ambrose in Aquinas, *Catena Aurea*, Luke 21:20-24.

111 St. Cyril understood lightning as a contrast linked to the warning about false messiahs. "His second coming shall not be in secret, but terrible and open. He shall descend in the glory of God the Father, with the Angels attending Him, to judge the world in righteousness. *Therefore He concludes, Go ye not therefore after them.*" Quoted in Aquinas, *Catena Aurea*, Luke 21:5-8.

attempt to build power and momentum as events develop. In contrast, the Second Advent will be like lightning: sudden, unmistakable, and uncontrollable. No one needs to tell you that lightning has struck. Even a blind man can hear the thunder that accompanies it.[112] Appropriately, Jesus is borrowing from the Psalms the idea of lightning as a herald of the Lord's coming.[113]

This brief answer in segment G' stands parallel to the question in segment G. Essentially, Jesus denies them any sign by pointing to lightning. Jesus *will* answer the second half of their question after the inclusio ends. But, here is the answer in a nutshell: The Second Advent will be sudden and unexpected.

A B C D E F G H I J K L M Z M' L' K' J' I' H' G' **F'** E' D' C' B' A'

Knowledge denied (24:28)

"Wherever the body is, there the eagles will be gathered together."

This is certainly an odd phrase; Segment F' seems to be out of place. In the Gospels, Jesus seldom mentions birds, yet this is the second "bird sighting" in the Olivet Discourse. Earlier, he spoke of gathering his people to protect and comfort them as does a mother hen. Here, he speaks of a bird that preys on dead flesh. What could this bird have to do with anything?

Looking at the chiasm we see that this phrase corresponds to parallel segment F, which is a question. The disciples get Jesus into a private setting and ask him for the inside scoop on the temple's destruction. Earlier, I asserted that what they

---

112 St. John Chrysostom, "For as the lightning needs no preacher nor messenger, but appears in a moment to all, so shall that advent be seen everywhere always to shine immediately." Quoted in Lapide, *The Great Commentary*, Matthew 24:27.

113 "Fire goes before him, and consumes his adversaries on every side. His lightnings light up the world; the earth sees and trembles . . . before the Lord of all the earth. The heavens proclaim his righteousness; and all the peoples behold his glory." Psalms 97:3-6.

want is information they can use to their advantage. In this, the disciples are not too different from the false messiahs. Each, in their own way, wants to control the events of Jerusalem's downfall—to get in front of the process. Jesus forcefully contradicts this mindset. They are not in control, *God is*.

This odd phrase in F' elucidates the control issue in corresponding segment F by alluding to an Old Testament story. The phrase about eagles appears in Job's encounter with God. Job was a wealthy and devout man in the Old Testament who, after a fairytale life, lost everything. Most of the book of Job revolves around conversations with his friends and with God, in which a central theme is control: Who should be in control of a man's life? Job had a common misconception: He believed that his success meant he was in control of his own destiny. He even demands, "Who is the Almighty, that we should serve him?" (Job 21:15). But, he learns his lesson when his life crashes and burns.

The eagles to which Jesus alludes are at the end of a long monologue in Job 38-39 wherein God reminds Job that *he* is infinite God, and man is merely a finite creature. God created the earth, the heavens, and everything in them. He alone controls all that he made. The passage starts with mention of the stars and the seas but goes on to show Job that he does not control even the lowly animals of nature. It ends with the example of the eagle (or vulture) that lives beyond the reach of mankind. The eagle feeds his young on the dead animals that Job has already been reminded are out of his control.

> "Is it at your command that the eagle mounts up and makes his nest on high? On the rock he dwells and makes his home in the fastness of the rocky crag. Thence he spies out the prey; his eyes behold it afar off. His young ones suck up blood; and *where the slain are, there is he*" (Job 39:26-30).

The odd phrase Jesus borrows should now be coming into focus. Man likes to pretend otherwise, but he cannot control his own personal destiny, much less the flow of history. We must learn the difficult lesson of Job in every generation. A diagnosis of cancer, an earthquake, a recalcitrant child, unemployment—many things can burst our secure little bubble. Only when we understand our own vulnerability do we begin to appreciate God's power.

To his credit, Job accepts the lesson. He admits he is not in control of his own destiny and that he was wrong to imply that God had been unfair.

> Job answered the LORD: "Behold, I am of small account; what shall I answer thee? I lay my hand on my mouth. I have spoken once . . . but I will proceed no further" (Job 40:3-5).

By alluding to the concluding phrase about eagles, Jesus invokes the conversation between God and Job.[114] The lesson that Job learned would be learned anew by the Christians in the destruction of Jerusalem. The false messiahs with their puny armies could not alter the course of the judgment determined by God. Jerusalem had rejected the true Messiah, and God's judgment was surely coming. Who is in control? Certainly not the Jews, not the disciples, and not even the Romans; it is God.[115]

Jesus wants his disciples to know that they are not in control, and that no amount of advance knowledge will change that. Nor should they follow the false messiahs. They may appear to be powerful and skillful, but they cannot control even

---

114   This was a common technique used in rabbinic argument, as well as by the New Testament writers.

115   This issue of control is made even clearer in the chiasm of Luke 17. There, it is the Pharisees claiming control, and Jesus using this phrase to deny it.

the birds of prey that will eat their flesh after battle. When will the temple be thrown down? It is not the issue of most consequence to you—events will play out in God's own time.

A B C D E F G H I J K L M Z M' L' K' J' I' H' G' F' E' D' C' B' A'

Falling (24:29)

"Immediately after the tribulation of those days the sun will be darkened, and the moon will not give its light, and the stars will fall from heaven, and the powers of the heavens will be shaken."

Now we are past the eight signs, past the repeated warnings about false messiahs, and we approach the judgment of Jerusalem itself. Since this was the topic of Jesus' statement in the ascending segment E, we would expect it again here. At first glance, though, it may seem that this is much more: Perhaps Jesus is speaking of the end of the world.

In fact, this is precisely what Russell, Schweitzer, and Lewis assumed: that the heavenly disruptions described here must entail the end of the world. Do they?

First, let us note the time frame. Jesus places the heavenly disruptions in the first century.[116] We already know that the Great Tribulation occurred during the persecution of Nero, and that the heavenly disruptions were to appear "immediately" thereafter.[117] There is no ambiguity to his statement, so was Jesus wrong?

To answer that question, it is essential to keep Jesus' words in their context of Old Testament prophecy. The words

---

116 This is how Luis Alcazar understood this part of the passage. In his commentary, *The Apocalypse*, he comments on 6:12, cited in Lapide, *The Great Commentary*, Matthew 24:29.

117 Luke 21:26 clearly places this event in the first century, as does Matthew. This is in agreement with St. Peter's view of Joel 2:31, as expounded in Acts 2:17. Interestingly, Mark 13:24 does not include the word *immediately*.

themselves, like so much of this discourse, are borrowed from the prophets, most specifically Isaiah, Ezekiel, Nahum, and Joel. Indeed, the more we read the prophets, the more familiar Jesus' words will sound. Note, for instance, the language of Isaiah as he predicts the destruction of Babylon:

> The stars of the heavens and their constellations will not give their light; the sun will be dark at its rising and the moon will not shed its light. . . . I will make the heavens tremble, and the earth will be shaken out of its place. Behold, I am stirring up the Medes against them (Isa. 13:9-17).

Babylon did fall to Cyrus and the Medo-Persian Empire, just as Isaiah had prophesied. Daniel 5 records the destruction of Belshazzar and the Babylonian court.

Isaiah used similar language to describe the overthrow of Edom.[118] Ezekiel used imagery every bit as vivid in his prophecy against Egypt.[119] Nahum used similar language to describe the destruction of Nineveh.[120]

Every one of these prophecies predicts heavenly disturbances. In every case, the ancient Jews believed that the prophecies had been fulfilled. Yet, in none of them did the sun, moon, and stars literally fall from the sky. None of the events occurred to herald the end of the whole world. All of them, however, did accompany the end of a *civilization*.

So, what is going on here? It is subtle, but not too complicated. All of these prophets used apocalyptic imagery: a

---

118   "All the host of heaven shall rot away, and the skies roll up like a scroll. All their host shall fall, as leaves fall from the vine." Isaiah 34:4-10.

119   "When I blot you out, I will cover the heavens, and make their stars dark; I will cover the sun with a cloud, and the moon shall not give its light. All the bright lights of heaven will I make dark over you, and put darkness upon your land, says the Lord God." Ezekiel 32:7-8.

120   "The mountains quake before him, the hills melt." Nahum 1:5.

language of calculated exaggeration. In apocalyptic literature, the destruction of an existing political order is often
described in astronomical terms. Kings and their court are
described as heavenly bodies. The falling stars, sun, and
moon are the kings, princes, and priests that fell in defeat.[121]

This can help us understand the additional details that
Luke adds to Matthew's account.

"There will be signs in the sun, the moon, and the stars,
and on the earth distress among nations confused by the
roaring of the sea and the waves. People will faint from
fear and foreboding of what is coming upon the world,
for the powers of the heavens will be shaken" (Luke
21:25–26).

The words added by Luke are a reflection of the prophet
Haggai. (St. Augustine wrote that Haggai was fulfilled in
the first century.)[122] The "sea" is a common scriptural metaphor for the Gentile nations.[123] "People will faint from fear"
because of the political storms buffeting the Roman Empire.

---

121 This can also be used as a positive analogy. In a divine promise of success we read, "Your sun
shall no more go down, nor your moon withdraw itself" (Isa. 30:26; also 60:19–20). Also,
"A star shall come forth out of Jacob, and a scepter shall rise out of Israel" (Num. 24:17).

122 An upheaval of all nations was predicted. "Thus says the Lord of hosts: Once again, in
a little while, I will shake the heavens and the earth and the sea and the dry land; and I
will shake all nations, so that the treasures of all nations shall come in, and I will fill this
house with splendor"(Hag. 2:6–7). Haggai was predicting the shaking, or overthrow,
of Jerusalem so that "the treasures of all nations," the Church, could be revealed. St.
Augustine wrote that the "splendor" was Christ, while the "house" was the Church.
See Augustine, *The City of God*, 18:48.

123 "The sea is a symbol of the Gentile nations. . . . It is a fitting symbol. The Gentile seas
have surged and raged around Israel for centuries, ever seeking to submerge her." John
Phillips, *Exploring Psalms: An Expository Commentary*, Volume 1, (Grand Rapids, MI,
Kregel Academic, 2002) 521. See also Currie, *Rapture*, 288–292, 358–359. Also Rev-
elation 13 read in light of Daniel 7; Revelation 21:1; Isaiah 17:12; 23:11; 57:20; 60:5;
Hosea 2:6–7; Matthew 13:47.

As already mentioned, some Romans thought that the empire was doomed in the upheaval following Nero's suicide.

This apocalyptic language would have been perfectly understandable to the first-century Jews. No one would have expected literal stars to fall out of the sky.[124] When we recognize it for what it is, we, too, can stop watching for the snuffing-out of the sun. We can understand the meaning of Jesus' words as originally intended.[125]

So, in segment E', Jesus consciously borrows apocalyptic language from the Old Testament. His disciples would have immediately understood him to be describing political upheaval, not the end of the world. Russell, Schweitzer, and Lewis were not acquainted with the literary styles of the ancient Jewish prophets, so they misunderstood the apocalyptic meaning. Jesus is speaking not of the end of the world but of the end of Jerusalem's civilization—the world *as the Jews knew it.*

Thus, the descending segment E' complements the ascending segment E. In E, Jesus predicts that the actual temple *building* will be destroyed. In E', Jesus further explains that not just the temple structure but also its entire *hierarchy* will be thrown down. This dovetails with the seven woes he has declared and is precisely what will happen in the first century when Jerusalem falls to the Romans.

---

124 This, of course, could not happen in any literal sense, even at the final eschaton, since stars are far larger than our earth.

125 Many of the Fathers focused on practical applications of passages. So, how they theoretically understood this may sometimes be murky. But St. Augustine clearly understood the sun, moon, and stars as symbols. He cited Song of Solomon 6:10, where sun and moon are used as symbols. Cited in Aquinas, *Catena Aurea,* Luke 21:25-27. Eusebius tied the darkening sun to St. Paul in 1 Corinthians 7:31, "the form of this world is passing away." We have already discussed this warning of St. Paul in segment J'. Cited in Aquinas, *Catena Aurea,* Matthew 24:37-39.

A B C D E F G H I J K L M Z M' L' K' J' I' H' G' F' E' D' C' B' A'

Appearing (24:30a)

"[T]hen will appear the sign of the Son of man in heaven."

By now, it should be apparent that Matthew was consistent in how he recorded the words of Jesus. Everything within the inclusio refers to the events of A.D. 70 when the temple was dismantled. The sole exception remains the contrast that Jesus made between the Second Advent in G' and the false messiahs in H'. And even this exception makes sense. Jesus was concerned about the false teachers and their coming assault on his flock of believers. They needed the contrast. It also allowed the chiasm to balance the question in segment G with a short answer in G'.

In ascending segment D, Jesus "left the temple . . . going away." Now, in segment D', his sign appears. The sides of the chiasm contrast with one another. Since D' follows directly on the heels of E', this sign should also be associated with the fall of Jerusalem's ruling class. It also directly precedes segment C', which speaks of the coming of the Son of Man. The context implies that Jesus was referring to A.D. 70, but what does it mean that the "sign of the Son of man" will "appear"? Were there any events that occurred around A.D. 70 that make sense of this statement? Also, is there any Old Testament mention of a heavenly sign to which Jesus might have been alluding?

Let's begin, as we should, with the Old Testament. There was another time in Israel's history when judgment fell upon Jerusalem. It was during the reign of King David, and we need to investigate this backdrop.

David had decided to number the people of Israel. Although a census may seem innocuous enough, it constituted a direct affront to the covenant that God had sworn to Abraham centuries earlier. God had asked Abraham to sacrifice his son Isaac on a mountain. When Abraham showed that he was willing, God stopped him, and swore a covenant with him. God declared, "I will indeed bless you, and I will make your offspring as numerous as the stars of heaven and as the sand that is on the seashore . . . because you have obeyed my voice" (Gen. 22:17-18).

No one tries to count the grains of sand on the beach. God was promising Abraham that his progeny would be innumerable.[126] Yet, when David was king, "Satan . . . provoked David to number Israel."[127] David was warned by his top general not to rebel against God with a census, but David ignored the warning. God's judgment followed swift and sure: A plague decimated Israel's populace.[128] The dire situation for David culminated at the same mountaintop spot on which Abraham had offered his son Isaac. In David's time, that mountain was owned by Oman the Jebusite. David encountered a heavenly angel there:

> God sent the angel to Jerusalem to destroy it . . . the angel of the LORD was standing by the threshing floor of Oman the Jebusite. . . . And David lifted his eyes and saw the angel of the LORD standing between earth and heaven, and *in his hand a drawn sword stretched out over Jerusalem* . . . he [David] was *afraid of the sword* of the angel of the LORD" (1 Chron. 21:14-30).

---

126 Compare the language of God's covenant with Genesis 41:49. Sand of the sea means "don't try to count."

127 1 Chronicles 21:1. The entire story is contained in 2 Samuel 24 and 1 Chronicles 21. Oman is called Araunah in Samuel.

128 God's prophet, Gad, had given King David a choice of three punishments.

Let us sum up this situation. The leader of Jerusalem (King David) obstinately disobeyed God. God sent judgment and a heavenly sign to accompany the judgment. An angel was part of that sign, but what frightened David was the heavenly sword that the angel wielded. The heavenly sword was a sign of God's judgment. (Even the Gentile Oman saw the sword and hid.)

Now, fast-forward to Jesus' day. The mount where David saw the sword is the foundation upon which the second temple stands. Jesus is teaching his disciples on the Mount of Olives, looking out at the temple mount where both Abraham and David had encountered God. He predicts that God's judgment will come upon Jerusalem's temple because Jerusalem's leadership has rejected God's plan for Israel—a rebellion even more egregious than David's. In this context, a sign similar to the sword that David saw might be expected.

According to the records of two different non-Christian historians, strange heavenly signs *did* appear at the time of Jerusalem's fall. One of the historians was Jewish—Josephus—while the other was the Roman historian Tacitus. Neither was particularly sympathetic to Christianity.

Now, I know what you may be thinking. "Those ancients were such naïve rubes, they would believe almost anything superstitious." But neither man was a fool. Both accepted the signs they recorded as factual only because of the large number of eyewitnesses. Conceding to his skeptical Roman readers that these events were hard to believe, Josephus wrote, "I suppose [this] account . . . would seem to be a fable, were it not related by those that saw it, and were not the events that followed it of so considerable a nature as to deserve such signals." Here is what the eyewitnesses saw, as related by Josephus:

There was *a star resembling a sword*, which stood over the city. . . . The men of learning understood it, that the security of their holy house was dissolved of its own accord. . . . So these publicly declared that *the signal foreshowed the desolation* that was coming upon them.[129]

He described other supernatural signs as well. Tacitus referred to a "fiery gleam of arms," which could easily correspond to Josephus' reference to a sword, and essentially confirms the thrust of Josephus.[130]

This sword that appeared in the heavens just before the temple was destroyed was similar to that which King David had seen a millennium earlier, in exactly the same location. Abraham offered Isaac on that mount. David saw the angel's sword and offered sacrifices on that mount. Solomon's temple was erected on that mount. Finally, that mount supported the second temple—the one that Jesus predicted would be torn down stone by stone.[131]

David had repented, and so God had stayed his angel of judgment. But in A.D. 70, the rulers of Jerusalem remained

---

129 There were other signs as well. "a comet, that continued a whole year. . . . Before the Jews' rebellion . . . so great a light shone round the altar and the holy house, that it appeared to be bright day time; which lasted for half an hour. . . . Moreover, the eastern gate of the inner court of the temple . . . was seen to be opened of its own accord about the sixth hour of the night. [This brass gate normally required 20 men to open and close it.] . . . Moreover, at that feast which we call Pentecost, as the priests were going by night into the inner court of the temple . . . they felt a quaking, and heard a great noise, and after that they heard a sound as of a great multitude, saying, 'Let us remove hence.'" Josephus, *Wars of the Jews,* 6, 5:3.

130 Tacitus wrote, "There had been seen hosts joining battle in the skies, *the fiery gleam of arms,* the temple illuminated by a sudden radiance from the clouds. The doors of the inner shrine were suddenly thrown open, and a voice of more than mortal tone was heard to cry that the gods were departing. At the same instant there was a mighty stir as of departure." Tacitus, *The Histories,* 5.

131 2 Chronicles 3:1: "Solomon began to build the house of the LORD in Jerusalem on Mount Moriah, where the LORD had appeared to David his father . . . on the threshing floor of Ornan the Jebusite." For more details, Scott Hahn, *A Father Who Keeps His Promises* (Ann Arbor, MI: Servant Books, 1998), 108.

obstinate to the very end. The sword of judgment was not turned away. Nevertheless, this "sign of the Son of man" appeared as a warning, as Jesus predicts here it will, when judgment falls on Jerusalem's leadership.

There is no good reason to doubt these eyewitnesses, other than our twenty-first-century rationalistic prejudices. Nor should our naturalistic prejudices blind us to what any first-century person would have understood immediately: A drawn sword with blade pointed down looks exactly like a Roman cross.[132]

The heavenly sword linked the temple's destruction to God's judgment. Most ancient Jews would have known the story of David and the heavenly sword. It was clear: The fall of Jerusalem was *God's* judgment. Today, Jews still commemorate that destruction on the ninth of Av (in mid-summer) every year, a solemn day called *Tisha B'Av.*

A B C D E F G H I J K L M Z M' L' K' J' I' H' G' F' E' D' C' B' A'

See the Son of Man (24:30b)

"[A]nd then all the tribes of the earth will mourn,
and they will see the Son of man coming on the clouds of heaven
with power and great glory."

Segment C' stands in contrast to ascending segment C, where Jesus declared that Jerusalem would "not see him again" until people greeted him with blessing. The blessings uttered at the triumphal entry were a very recent memory,

---

132 St. Cyril of Jerusalem, "Christ's own true sign is the Cross. . . . The sign of the Cross shall be a terror to His foes; but joy to His friends who have believed in Him." Cyril, *Catechetical Lectures of St. Cyril,* 15:22; trans., Edwin Hamilton Gifford, *Nicene and Post-Nicene Fathers,* vol. 7 (Oxford: Parker, 1893). Also, the Church sings in the ancient office for Holy Cross Day, "This sign of the cross shall be in heaven when the Lord shall come to judgment."

and Jesus predicted in C that they would happen again.[133] But C' must be referring to a different coming, because here the tribes who "see the Son of man" will be in *mourning*.

There is a great deal of content in this segment. And we have finally arrived at the very crux of the controversy with Russell, Schweitzer, and Lewis. So, before we look at the passage itself, it behooves us to examine what the word *coming* means. This is not meant as a dodge. Jesus assumed so much background in this discourse that we need to bring our own thinking up to speed.

Different kinds of coming

The "coming" of Jesus has more than one connotation. This multitude of connotations has a long pedigree that finds its origin in Aramaic, the common language spoken in Jesus' day. Christians still use some Aramaic, as in the common exclamation *maranatha*. Although we use this as one word, it is actually a phrase of two words—one phrase that can mean two different things, depending on how the Aramaic words are divided within it. Of course, the New Testament was originally written down with no spaces at all, which means this ambivalence of meaning was inherent in the original text of the Bible.

If the words are read as *marana tha*, the meaning is an exclamation of hope: "Lord, come!" constituting an entreaty directed at the future.[134] But if the third letter *a* is attached to the final syllable, it reads *maran atha*. Now the meaning

---

133 Matthew 21:7-9 relates the triumphal entry. "They brought the ass and the colt, and put their garments on them, and [Jesus] sat thereon. . . . And the crowds that went before him and that followed him shouted, 'Hosanna to the Son of David! Blessed is he who comes in the name of the Lord! Hosanna in the highest!'"

134 "Christians pray, above all in the Eucharist, to hasten Christ's return by saying to him: Maranatha! 'Our Lord, come!'" CCC, 671. Also I Corinthians 11:26 and 16:22; 2 Peter 3:11-12; Revelation 22:17-20.

is a statement of faith—"the Lord has come"—a definitive word of history, a declaration of a past event. So, within the Aramaic of the New Testament, there is reference to at least two comings. *Maranatha* speaks both to the sure hope of the Second Advent in the future and as a declaration of the Incarnation, the coming of Jesus within history. Between these two poles of meaning are other comings, which we need to discuss.

Pope Benedict XVI has pointed out that the idea of multiple comings of Christ can be found in the catechesis of St. Cyril of Jerusalem.[135] He tells us that the concept was further developed by St. Bernard of Clairvaux, who mentioned a third coming between the more commonly acknowledged First and Second Advents. Citing John's Gospel, Bernard wrote: "Jesus answered him, 'If a man loves me, he will keep my word, and my Father will love him, and *we will come to him* and make our home with him'" (John 14:23). This intermediate coming—or middle coming—is Christ's continual coming in his Church.[136]

Seven centuries before Bernard, Augustine taught multiple comings of Christ; so much so that it can be called an integral part of his thinking. We touched briefly on this in

---

135 St. Cyril mentions two Advents. Cyril, *Catechetical Lectures of St. Cyril*, 15:1-3. Also, Pope Benedict, *Jesus of Nazareth: From the Entrance Into Jerusalem To The Resurrection* (Ignatius Press, San Francisco, CA, 2011) 289-292.

136 "We know that there are three comings of the Lord. The third lies between the other two. It is invisible, while the other two are visible. In the first coming he was seen on earth. . . . In the final coming all flesh will see the salvation of our God. . . . The *intermediate coming is a hidden one*; in it only the elect see the Lord within their own selves, and they are saved. In his first coming our Lord came in our flesh and in our weakness; in *this middle coming* he comes in spirit and in power; in the final coming he will be seen in glory and majesty. In case someone should think that what we say about *this middle coming* is sheer invention, listen to what our Lord himself [said]." This is contained in the Office of Readings for Wednesday of the First Week of Advent, in *Liturgy of the Hours* (Totowa, NJ: Catholic Book Publishing, 1975). It comes from Bernard of Clairvaux, *Adventu Domini*, Sermon 5:1, cited by Pope Benedict, *Jesus of Nazareth: From the Entrance Into Jerusalem To The Resurrection*, 289-292.

segment F when we examined the two questions contained in three clauses that began this discourse. Here is the full quote that we edited previously, with bracketed numbers added to emphasize the three clauses—rather than the two answers—in the original question of the disciples:

For the Lord gave these replies to the disciples who asked him what was going to follow after that time, whether about [1] the destruction of Jerusalem, the topic that occasioned the questions, or about [2] his coming through the Church, in which he does not cease to come until the end. For we recognize him as he comes in his own members when they are daily born. . . . Since, then, he mentions signs that refer to these three, that is, to [1] the destruction of that city, to [2] his coming in his own body, which is the Church, and to [3] his coming as head of the Church [at the eschaton], which he is himself, we must distinguish through careful consideration which of those signs refers to which of those three events. Otherwise we might suppose that what pertains to [1] the destruction of Jerusalem refers to [3] the end of the world. Or just the opposite, we might state that what pertains to [3] the end of the world refers to [1] the destruction of that city. Or we might say that what pertains to [2] his coming in his body, because he is the Church, refers to [3] his last coming in his body, which is the head of the Church. Or again, we might claim that what pertains to [3] his last coming by himself refers to [2] his coming through the Church.[137]

Notice the second clause references multiple comings. Since "coming" can reference so many different events, Au-

---

137 St. Augustine, *The Works of Saint Augustine*, Epistle 199, 340:25-26.

gustine urged caution, the reasons for which Russell and Schweitzer were oblivious:

> Many passages . . . though they seem to refer to the last judgment . . . allude rather to some other event—whether to that coming of the Savior which continually occurs in His Church . . . or to *the destruction of the earthly Jerusalem*.[138]

Aquinas expanded on Augustine, pointing to these multiple comings of Christ as a key to understanding the Gospels. I have inserted bracketed numbers to match the numbers in Augustine's quote above.

> The signs of which we read in the gospels, as Augustine says . . . refer not only [3] to Christ's coming to judgment, but also [1] to the time of *the sack of Jerusalem*, and [2] to the coming of Christ in ceaselessly visiting His Church. So that, perhaps, if we consider them carefully, we shall find that none of them refers to the coming advent.[139]

The same three clauses are there, but St. Thomas switches the order.

It should be clear where this line of reasoning is headed, but let's back up a moment and follow the argument in detail. Pope Benedict fleshes out the concept, enumerating multiple comings of Christ.[140] He does not list them out as I have below, but if we read him carefully, we can detect in his writings seven different "comings" of Jesus:

---

138 St. Augustine, *The City of God,* 20.

139 Thomas Aquinas, *Summa Theologica*, trans. Fathers of the English Dominican Province (Chicago, IL: Benzinger Brothers, 1947), Supplement Q 73:1.

140 Pope Benedict, *Jesus of Nazareth: From the Entrance Into Jerusalem To The Resurrection*, 289-292.

1. Christ comes in the flesh—the Incarnation.
2. Christ comes in the sacraments—especially in the Eucharist.
3. Christ comes in the Word—Holy Scripture read in community.
4. Christ comes in his Spirit—all throughout salvation history.
5. Christ comes in holy people—the saints of salvation history.
6. Christ comes in judgment—the various events of history.
7. Christ comes in glory—the glory of the Second Advent at the final eschaton.

The first and most obvious coming was the *Incarnation* two millennia ago. The Second Person of the Holy Trinity emptied himself and came as a man to blaze a way back to God for us. All the other comings are contingent upon this first one.

The seventh and last coming is the glorious hope of all Christians: *Christ will come again* to close the curtain on history. That coming will usher our reality into eternity. It is the event to which all creation is yearning. Christians anticipate it with hope; sinners look to it with fear; atheists view it with scorn.

Here is where the skeptics go awry. They assume that when Jesus spoke of coming again, he was speaking always and only of that final event. But there are at least five additional comings of Jesus that Pope Benedict XVI labels as the "middle comings." As noted above, St. Augustine wrote that Christ is always coming to his Church.[141]

The *sacraments* are a true coming of Jesus to his people, and they represent the second coming on this list. He comes to dwell within the soul at the sacrament of baptism. He marks the soul permanently in confirmation and holy orders. The supreme example of this coming is evident in the

---

141   Additional references to this in St. Augustine, quoted in Aquinas, *Catena Aurea*, Matthew 24:6-8; Luke 21:25-27.

Eucharist. Christ comes to dwell within his people: body, soul, blood, and divinity.

While the consecration happens during the second half of the Mass, Christ also comes to us in the first half of the Mass. He comes to us in *word*, the third coming in our list. We stand out of respect when the Gospel is read, because Christ is truly present in his word.

The fourth coming is closely related to the second and third: Christ comes in *spirit*. This coming (along with the next two) partially predates the other comings in salvation history, for the spirit of God came upon the prophets at certain times. But since Christ's Incarnation and his Ascension to his Father, the coming of Christ's spirit has a new vitality. All Christians experience this coming of Christ, for he has made a solemn promise that wherever his believers gather, he will be in their "midst"—he will come in spirit (Matt. 18:20).

The fifth and sixth comings of Christ are similar in that they both involve the coming of Christ in and through something else. The fifth is the coming of Christ in the *lives of great saints*. (The pope mentions two examples, Francis and Dominic.) These saints truly represent Christ's coming into the world to shape human history—it is more than just a metaphorical "coming." This was a concept familiar to the Jews of Jesus' day. They said, "A great prophet has appeared among us. . . . God has *come* to help his people" (Luke 7:16, NIV).

The sixth coming is the most important of the middle comings for our discussion of the Olivet Discourse: Christ comes in *events*. Although Pope Benedict may have had both joyous and difficult events in mind, we will focus on "judgment" events. God can and does come in his judgment upon a people. As noted already, both Augustine and Aquinas mentioned this type of coming when they referred to the destruction of Jerusalem.

The Old Testament repeatedly speaks of this type of "judgment coming" as a true coming. God warns his people so that they can recognize him in the judgment when it arrives. For example, Isaiah predicts the destruction of Egypt by the Assyrians: "The Lord is riding on a swift cloud and comes to Egypt; and the idols of Egypt will tremble at his presence" (Isa. 19:1-2, cf. 20:1-6). Shortly thereafter, we read of the fulfillment of this prophecy. Nowhere in the passage, nor in the historical records, is there any mention of unusual "swift cloud" formations: God did not make himself visible to Egypt in any physical manifestation. None, that is, except in the Assyrian army! That army was the embodiment of God's judgment. God came gloriously in judgment on clouds, but what was seen physically was the Assyrian army. The eye of faith saw God's coming in that destructive army. It was a true coming, as God had predicted through his prophet.

Ezekiel used language similar to that of Isaiah to predict that God would send Babylon to destroy Egypt. In his prophecy against Egypt he said, "The day of the Lord is near; it will be a day of clouds" (Ezek. 30:3). Notice that Ezekiel used "day of the Lord" language. Some have mistakenly believed that the "day of the Lord" always refers to the final eschaton. But Ezekiel obviously does not use it that way. The "day of the Lord" here refers to the end of the world *as Egypt knew it.*

In Daniel, we encounter the coming of God in judgment once again. The ruler within Babylon was Belshazzar. While partying, he ordered his servants to use the sacred vessels that his grandfather had plundered from the Jerusalem temple. In response to this sacrilege, "the fingers of a man's hand appeared and wrote on the plaster of the wall. . . . And the king saw the hand as it wrote" (Dan. 5:5).

Understandably, a hand without a body freaked out the king. Daniel interpreted the handwriting: "God has num-

bered the days of your kingdom and brought it to an end."
Daniel's choice of words is important. Who ended the reign
of the Babylonian king? God did. Belshazzar was judged by
God because he did "not honor" him (Dan. 5:23-26).

This story in Daniel ends with the slaying of Belshazzar. We read that Darius the Mede "received the kingdom"
(Dan. 5:31). Although an uninformed observer might have
thought that the Medo-Persian army ended Belshazzar's
kingdom, the reader of Daniel understands a deeper truth.
God had come in judgment on Belshazzar because of his sacrilege, and a new king received the kingdom. This "judgment coming" was real in spite of the fact that God never
actually met with either king in any sort of physical way; in
spite of the fact that Darius the Mede was not even a believer
in the God of Israel (at least not at that point).

This is a critical concept. When the Assyrian army dev-
astated Egypt, when the Babylonian army defeated Egypt,
when the Medo-Persian army conquered Babylon—each
event was predicted by a prophet so that devout men would
know that it was *God's coming in judgment.*

Jesus appropriated this language and these concepts, as
did his disciples. For example, in the book of Revelation,
Jesus warns the unrepentant Church in Ephesus that he will
"come to you and remove your lampstand." A few verses
later, Jesus also warns of his coming to "make war" against
some within the Church in Pergamum. A little later, he
warns the Church in Sardis, saying that he will come in
judgment at a time they could not predict (cf. Rev. 2:5-3:3).
The context in all three instances is clear: Christ was speaking of a middle coming in judgment, not about the Second
Advent at the end of the world.[142]

---

142 Portions of Revelation speak to the Second Advent, but its main message is about the

By now, it should be evident that to make sense of scriptural prophecy, we must not assume that every "coming" predicted in the New Testament refers to the Second Advent. As both Augustine and Aquinas reminded us, we must look at the context of each statement, and the context of the entire Bible, to determine the intended meaning.

The trial

Jesus spoke of "coming" at least twice within just a few days of his Passion. The first was in the Olivet Discourse we have been examining. The other time was at his trial before the Sanhedrin a few days later. We need to examine this trial to cement our understanding of these concepts.

At his trial, the high priest solemnly asked Jesus if he was the Messiah. Jesus replied, "I tell you, hereafter you will see the Son of man seated at the right hand of Power, and *coming* on the clouds of heaven" (Matt. 26:64).

In the time of Jesus, this phrase *son of man* was ambiguous, potentially meaning one of three things. First, the phrase was commonly used to designate oneself as a "Joe Average Jew." Jesus used this phrase of himself repeatedly during his public ministry, and his hearers might very well have assumed this to be his meaning.[143]

---

middle coming in judgment on Jerusalem. See Scott Hahn, *Lamb's Supper*, (New York: Doubleday Religion, 1999), 93. Also, Michael Barber, *Coming Soon: Unlocking the Book of Revelation and Applying Its Lessons Today*, (Steubenville, OH: Emmaus Road Publishing, 2006). Also, Currie, *Rapture*, 221-372, 451-463.

143 That ambiguity is evident, for example, in Psalms 8, where son of man can be understood as speaking of mankind in general. Alternatively, Psalms 8 can be understood as a Messianic psalm speaking of Christ and the son of man Incarnated. "When I look at thy heavens, the work of thy fingers, the moon and the stars which thou hast established; what is man that thou art mindful of him, and the son of man that thou dost care for him? Yet thou hast made him little less than God, and dost crown him with glory and honor." John Bergsma, "Mountains and Mediators: A Survey of the Old Testament," class lectures at Franciscan University available on CD (Harahan, LA: Catholic Productions, 2010).

Second, *son of man* could refer to the Israelites in the context of their relationship to God. There is no need to understand this sense of *son of man* as anything out of the ordinary, either. It would designate "Joe Average Jew" as one of "God's chosen people."[144]

But when Jesus stood before the Sanhedrin, he purposely eliminated any ambiguity in this phrase. He could only have been referring to the third meaning: the kingly-priestly messiah figure of the Old Testament; the Anointed One of God. How did he do that? Jesus made his meaning clear by placing the "Son of man" title in the context of Psalm 110 and Daniel 7.

In the vision of Daniel, four beasts appear that represent four kingdoms. Without getting into the details, this fourth kingdom has traditionally been understood to be the Roman Empire.[145] During the time of the fourth kingdom, the "Son of man" appears and is given an eternal kingdom that surpasses all earthly kingdoms. Notice the similarity to the language that Jesus used at his trial.

> I saw in the night visions, and behold, with *the clouds of heaven there came one like a son of man*, and he came to the Ancient of Days and was presented before him. And to him was given dominion and glory and kingdom, that all peoples, nations, and languages should serve him; his dominion is an everlasting dominion, which shall not pass away, and his kingdom one that shall not be destroyed (Dan. 7:13-14).

This son of man in Daniel is portrayed as a high priestly figure who is also a king. He is presented before God, the

---

144 For example, in Psalms 80:17, "But let thy hand be upon the man of thy right hand, the son of man whom thou hast made strong for thyself!"

145 For a thorough treatment of the four kingdoms, see Currie, *Rapture*, 85-103.

Ancient of Days, as a priest. He is given dominion over an eternal kingdom as a king. This occurs during the reign of the fourth kingdom (Rome).

Notice that there is indeed a "coming" spoken of here in Daniel. The Son of Man is pictured as coming with the clouds of heaven. The direction of this coming is important. The Son travels *toward* the Ancient of Days—toward God—not toward man. In other words, the *terminus ad qualm* of the coming in Daniel's vision is heaven, not earth. The Son of Man is presented to God in heaven as priest, and is given authority to reign forever as king.

So, we can be sure that Daniel's scene of coming does not describe the Second Coming. The direction of travel precludes it. Also, it is to occur during the fourth kingdom—the Roman Empire—not at the end of the world. Since Jesus borrows from Daniel's vision when he answers the Sanhedrin, he must not be referring to the Second Advent, either.

Jesus also alludes to Psalm 110 at his trial. "The Lord says to my lord: 'Sit at my right hand, till I make your enemies your footstool'" (110:1).[146]

Although the picture envisioned is similar to Daniel's, there are two additional things we can glean here. Not only does the Son of Man "come" and receive the kingdom, he is seated in victory at the right hand of God: the position of power and trust. This makes Jesus' meaning even clearer: He is not telling the high priest that he is "Joe Average Jew"—he is claiming that it is *he* who will sit upon the messianic throne of David in the kingdom. It is *he* who will approach God's throne as priest and sit at God's right hand as king.

---

146 Because of the similarity in subject matter and language, the Church has long connected Daniel 7 and Psalm 110. An example is Lactantius, the Christian Cicero of the fourth century. See Lanctantius, *The Epitome of the Divine Institutes*, 47; in Roberts, *Ante-Nicene Fathers*.

Jesus could not have been referring to his Second Advent: He is seated in heaven, not coming to earth.

Further, while Jesus is seated, his enemies will be conquered—made into his "footstool." At the moment Jesus speaks these words, he is standing in chains on trial for his life. The Sanhedrin would naturally have assumed that Jesus meant to identify them—the Jewish leadership—as the enemies alluded to in the psalm. Jesus would sit at the right hand of God while they were being conquered.

This is the third reason that Jesus could not have been speaking of the final eschaton when he spoke at his trial. Psalm 110 speaks of his enemies being conquered *after* his coming and *while* he is seated. In other words, the coming of Psalm 110 had to happen within time, not at the end of time.

This, of course, fits perfectly with the Church's understanding of its own character.[147] The Church is both now and not yet. The kingdom has been founded, yet we still pray daily for its coming. It is both victorious, at rest in heaven, and yet still militant, working for victory here on earth. The heavenly reality is that the victory over the enemies of Christ is assured.

How can victory be so assured? Because Daniel tells us, and Jesus repeats, that he "will come with the clouds of heaven." The Old Testament prophets spoke of *God's* coming on clouds. When Jesus predicts his own return on

---

147 "Though already present in his Church, Christ's reign is nevertheless yet to be fulfilled 'with power and great glory' by the King's return to earth." *Catechism of the Catholic Church* (New York: Doubleday Religion, 2003), 671 (hereafter *Catechism*). "The kingdom of Christ [is] now present in mystery.""In the presence of Christ, this kingdom was clearly open to the view of men. . . . The Miracles of Jesus also confirm that the Kingdom has already arrived on earth. . . . While it slowly grows, the Church strains toward the completed Kingdom and, with all its strength, hopes and desires to be united in glory with its King."*Dogmatic Constitution on the Church, Lumen Gentium*: Second Vatican Council (Vatican, 1964), 3 and 5.

clouds, he is laying claim to a prerogative of God himself.[148] He will come in glory to judge. The Sanhedrin is not dealing with a mere prophet at their trial. Jesus is claiming *divine* authority because of *who he is*.

Jesus adds an essential note that should have struck terror into the hearts of those who heard him. Christ rolls Daniel and Psalms together and proclaims that the very men that are sitting in judgment before him would witness his victory. Daniel's fourth beast (Rome) might survive for another few centuries; but the Son of Man will be seated in victory next to the Ancient of Days, at the right hand of Power, during the generation of that Sanhedrin.

There could be little doubt about his meaning. It is a warning. Jesus is claiming to be the priestly-kingly Messiah with divine prerogatives. He is assuring his captors that they will know this to be true . . . before they die. He will be viewed as the victor during their lifetimes. Yet at this moment he stands before them as a prisoner in chains, about to be judged as deserving of death.

Did the high priest and the Sanhedrin understand all of this imagery from Psalms and Daniel? You bet they did! They knew their scriptures. They understand him perfectly. Immediately after this statement of Jesus, the high priest rends his garment—a sign that he believes he is hearing blasphemy. The Sanhedrin then sets about finding a way to execute Jesus.

Can we summarize? By borrowing from Daniel and Psalms, Jesus makes it clear that the "coming on the clouds of heaven" does not refer to his Second Advent. First, it cannot,

---

148 St. John Chrysostom, "God ever appears in a cloud, according to Psalms [17]. . . . Therefore shall the Son of man come in the clouds as God." Chrysostom, in Aquinas, *Catena Aurea*, Luke 21:25-27.

because Christ will be traveling toward the Ancient of Days, not toward the Mount of Olives. Secondly, the passages never have him on earth but rather seated in heaven. Furthermore, the Psalms passage clearly refers to activity against enemies during time that comes after the coming; but the final eschaton will be the last event in time. Finally, in Daniel's vision this all occurs during the time of the fourth kingdom (Rome), and Jesus shortens that time frame to a single generation.

One final question remains: Was Jesus' prophecy fulfilled?

Did that generation of the Sanhedrin witness any event that would have been irrefutable proof that they had erred in rejecting Jesus as their messianic king? Did Jesus return to sit at the right hand of the Ancient of Days? Did Christ come in judgment to the Sanhedrin as he predicted at his trial?

The answer is an unqualified "yes" to all. In less than six weeks, Jesus would ascend to his Father and sit at his right hand.[149] His disciples were his witnesses. But there was a more public event less than four decades after the trial and Passion. Jerusalem revolted against the Roman Empire; consequently the Romans conquered Jerusalem and destroyed the temple forever. The Sanhedrin disappeared from history, never to return. Christ's prediction at his trial is a promise to *come in judgment* of his captors—a promise that he kept.

Back to the Olivet Discourse

Now that we have reviewed the language and allusions Jesus employed at his trial, we can return to the Olivet Discourse, which preceded the Sanhedrin trial by a few days.[150] The context of the discourse should be coming into clear focus

---

149 This is also the meaning of Matthew 10:23.
150 This discourse occurred approximately three days before the Passion. Lapide, *The Great Commentary*, Matthew 23:38.

now: Jesus warns his disciples about his coming in judgment, then he warns the Sanhedrin at his trial. Both warnings refer to the same event, a middle coming in judgment. Both of them have a context that precludes understanding them as a reference to the Second Coming.

Now, perhaps, we can understand why St. Augustine spoke clearly of more than two "comings," especially with regard to the Olivet Discourse:

> Many passages . . . seem to refer to the last judgment, yet on a closer examination they are found to be ambiguous, or to allude rather to some other event—whether to that coming of the Savior which continually occurs in His Church . . . *or to the destruction of the earthly Jerusalem* . . . [these] events cannot be distinguished unless all the corresponding passages bearing on the subject in the three evangelists, Matthew, Mark, and Luke, are compared with one another—for some things are put more obscurely by one evangelist and more plainly by another—so that it becomes apparent what things are meant to be referred to one event.[151]

As we already saw, St. Thomas agreed. Jesus came at the Incarnation, then returned in victory to his Father at the Ascension, but *came and judged* the Sanhedrin within that generation.

Segment C' contains the core of misunderstanding for Russell, Schweitzer, Lewis, and our Catholic college student. They assumed—along with many other Christians and skeptics—that Jesus is mistakenly predicting his Second Coming in glory within a very short time. Now we have seen this is not the case. We should have guessed, since all of the signs

---

151 Augustine, *The City of God*, 20:4–5.

that he gave to his disciples in the rest of this passage also occurred within their generation. We should have known, since the inclusio marks out the single answer about the temple. We should have paid attention, since the chiasm makes it rather clear. Jesus is still answering the initial question of the disciples, "When will the temple be destroyed?" We now know the answer: The destruction of the temple will happen during Christ's *middle coming in judgment* in A.D. 70.

Remember what we learned about the coming in judgment: It is a true coming, even without any visual or physical manifestation of God. When Assyria conquered Egypt, it was God coming in judgment—but the Egyptians saw an Assyrian army. In like manner, the Sanhedrin saw the Roman army sent by Caesar Nero. If we knew the Old Testament as well as the ancient Jews did, we would have recognized immediately that "the Son of man coming on the clouds of heaven with power and great glory" referred to Daniel's vision and did not fit the scenario of the Second Coming.

None of this should surprise the faithful Catholic. In its liturgy, the Church does not connect Daniel 7 to the Second Advent, but rather to the Transfiguration.[152] Peter, James, and John experienced the transcendence of Jesus Christ, which helped them to understand who Jesus really was. It prepared them for Jesus' otherworldly claims about the Eucharist. It prepared them for the Ascension from that same mount. And it prepared them to accept the middle comings of Christ as true comings of God after his Resurrection.

Indeed, at the Transfiguration, Jesus also uses "middle coming" language:

---

152 On August 6, we celebrate the Feast of the Transfiguration of the Lord. Daniel 7:9-14 is read every year; while the Transfiguration accounts in Matthew 17:1-9, Mark 9:2-10, and Luke 9:28-36 rotate in the three-year cycle.

"For the Son of man is to come with his angels in the glory of his Father, and then he will repay every man for what he has done. Truly, I say to you, there are some standing here who will not taste death before they see the Son of man coming in his kingdom" (Matt. 16:27-28).

The mention of the angels should remind us of the Olivet Discourse. In the upcoming segment B', Christ "will send out his angels with a loud trumpet call." We will examine it shortly. But for now, when would he repay the Sanhedrin for being blind guides leading Israel astray? It will be at the judgment of A.D. 70. And as Jesus predicts, one of the disciples present on the mount—John—will be alive to witness it.

Mourning

Although this answers the central question of segment C', there is still a bit more to unpack. What can we make of Jesus' statement that "all the tribes of the earth will mourn"? Did that occur, too?

First of all, we need to examine the translation of this sentence. The Greek word for *earth* is *ge*, and it can be used in different ways. This is not unique to Greek. In English we use *earth* to mean the globe on which all humanity resides, and we use the same word to refer to a shovelful of dirt. In Scripture, *ge* can refer to the planet, but it can also refer to the land within the territorial boundaries of Israel. The antonym of "earth" in the sense of "land of Israel" would be the "sea," referring to the Gentile nations—all that territory not a part of Israel. (Of course, sea in its other meaning designates an expansive body of water.)

In the Bible, this second meaning of *ge*—land of Israel—is actually the more common use of the word, and it certainly makes Jesus' words here more understandable. He tells us that "all the tribes of the land will mourn." The tribes, it is now clear, would be the tribes of Israel. For this prophecy to be fulfilled the entire planet need not mourn over the events in Jerusalem—just the Jewish people. And once again these words of Jesus allude to an Old Testament prediction. Zechariah prophesied that on "that day," "the inhabitants of Jerusalem . . . when they look on him whom they have pierced, they shall mourn for him" (12:10).[153]

So what can history tell us? There were three walls that protected Jerusalem. Even after the Romans had breached the first two, the Jews stood on top of the last wall and mocked the Roman soldiers. They shouted that "this temple would be preserved by him that inhabited therein [God], whom they still had for their assistant in this war, and did therefore laugh at all his [General Titus's] threatenings, which would come to nothing, because the conclusion of the whole depended upon God only."[154] The Jews in Jerusalem were certain that God would protect his beloved city and temple. Shortly thereafter, they came to the grisly realization that God would not defend them any longer—surely the greatest-imaginable reason for a Jew to mourn.

Their defeat was also proof that God had used the Romans to judge them. The destruction of the temple was public evidence that Jesus was the spiritual victor over the Old Covenant's failed leadership. Even the pagan population of the Roman Empire connected the dots between the fates of Jesus and Jerusalem. For example, Mara Bar Serapion, a Syrian Gentile, wrote a letter to his son sometime after A.D. 73 encouraging him to work against injustice:

---

153 For a detailed discussion of Zechariah, see Currie, *Rapture*, 431–450.
154 Josephus, *Wars of the Jews*, 5, 11:2.

What advantage did the Athenian gain from putting Socrates to death? Famine and plague came upon them as a judgment for their crime.

What advantage did the men of Samos gain from burning Pythagoras? In a moment their land was covered with sand.

What advantage did the Jews gain from executing their wise King? It was just after that that their kingdom was abolished.

God justly avenged these three wise men.[155]

If Mara Bar Serapion figured this out, we can be sure the Jewish "tribes of the land" figured it out, and mourned bitterly. They had missed the visitation of their king, Jesus Christ. Their God no longer protected them, but rather judged them with destruction.

A B C D E F G H I J K L M Z M' L' K' J' I' H' G' F' E' D' C' **B'** **A'**

Gathering successful (24:31)

"[A]nd he will send out his angels with a loud trumpet call,
and they will gather his elect from the four winds,
from one end of heaven to the other."

Once again Jesus invokes a rich background of meaning from the Old Testament, in which the "four winds of heaven" is a relatively common image. When God providen-

---

155 Mara Bar Serapion, quoted in Frederick Fyvie Bruce, *The New Testament Documents, Are They Reliable?* (Downers Grove, IL: Intervarsity Press, 1972), 172.

tially disperses a people from their ancestral lands, it is often described as being scattered to the "four winds" of heaven. Jeremiah predicted this fate upon Elam, and then defined his meaning by stating "there shall be no nation to which those driven out of Elam shall not come" (Jer. 49:36). It can happen even to political dynasties, such as the splitting of the kingdom of Alexander the Great, which Daniel describes as "divided toward the four winds of heaven" (Dan. 11:4). In neither of these occasions do the prophets have an otherworldly focus—the reference to "four winds of heaven" simply underscores God's thoroughness in scattering.[156]

But God does not only scatter, he also re-gathers his people after tribulation. He is not the God of judgment only, but the God of love and mercy. When God restores his people, the Old Testament says he is gathering them *from* the four winds of heaven.[157]

Here in the Olivet Discourse, Jesus' words reflect the re-gathering language we find in Ezekiel's vision of the dry bones. "Come from the four winds, O breath . . . and the breath came into them, and they lived" (Ezek. 37:9-14). In this passage, God resurrects a valley of dry bones. Ezekiel uses this resurrection imagery to predict the spiritual rejuvenation and re-gathering of the Israelites in the New Exodus after the Babylonian exile. In the First Exodus, Moses led them from slavery in Egypt. In the New Exodus, Ezekiel promised that God's people would be re-gathered for renewal even though they were coming "from the four winds." Ezekiel's message gave hope to the people of God during the Babylonian exile, because they had been scattered. Scattering was a consequence of sin.[158]

---

156 St. Bede, "By 'the four winds' he means the four parts of the world; the east, the west, the north and the south." Bede in Aquinas, *Catena Aurea*, Mark 13:21-27.

157 See Zechariah 2:6, Isaiah 11:12.

158 Ever since the Tower of Babel, scattering is considered a judgment for sin (see Genesis

Here, in the Olivet Discourse, Jesus knows that his Church is about to experience a scattering. It was Old Israel that precipitated it by rejecting their Messiah, not New Israel, but nonetheless, the Church is to be scattered; so Jesus offers a word of hope. After warning the disciples about tribulation, heresy, flight, scattering, and destruction, Jesus predicts the revitalization and reunification of his young Church. By A.D. 70, Christians will be plagued with Jewish and Roman persecutions; and in fleeing Jerusalem (at the behest of Jesus himself) they will be dispersed throughout the known world. But here Jesus promises that they will be re-gathered and unified under his protection.

In the ascending segment B, Jesus bemoaned the resistance of the Jews to his attempts at gathering them for their own protection. Here in B', Christ sends out his angels, who are successful at gathering his new people, the Church, from their worldwide scattering.[159] The contrast is clear: This time, God's people will *want* to be gathered.

Why are they being gathered? The Church is being re-gathered to celebrate the *yovel*—the Jubilee. How do we know that? When the Hebrew word *yovel* was translated into the Greek Septuagint, it became "a trumpet blast of liberty." By speaking of sending messengers abroad with a "loud trumpet call," Jesus is making the allusion unmistakable.[160] Compare Christ's language to that of Moses instituting the Jubilee celebration:

11:4-9).

159 St. Augustine, "He will send his angels, and from the four corners of the world, that is from the whole world, he will gather his chosen ones." Augustine, *The Works of Saint Augustine*, Epistle 199, 349:44.

160 In fact, some Greek manuscripts of Matthew mirror the Greek Septuagint of Leviticus in word usage: *salpiggos phones* and *salpiggosphonei.*

"Then *you shall send abroad the loud trumpet* on the . . . Day of Atonement. *You shall send abroad the trumpet throughout all your land.* And you shall . . . proclaim liberty throughout the land to all its inhabitants; it shall be a jubilee for you" (Lev. 25:9-14).[161]

What was a Jubilee? It was based on the seven-year Sabbatical cycle—the *shemittah.* Every seventh year, the law required a year of rest for all workers and all land in Israel, as well as forgiveness of all debt.[162] Then every seventh *shemittah* (every forty-nine years) a fiftieth Jubilee year was to be proclaimed—the *yovel.* Added to the *shemittah* requirements were two additional Jubilee obligations: the release of all slaves and the restoration of all ancestral lands to their original tribes.[163] By making society abide by rules of justice and forgiveness, the Jubilee "incarnated" the forgiveness of God into the social structure of Israel.[164] Between the time of Moses and Jesus, the Jubilee developed into a triple-themed concept: forgiveness, restoration, and liberty.[165]

---

161 The Day of Atonement was a new beginning in that all prior year's sins were forgiven. The high priest recreated Israel as she was intended to be: a visible presence of God on earth. See Margaret Barker, *Risen Lord: Scottish Journal of Theology* (Edinburgh: T&T Clark, 1996), 61-64.

162 We are abbreviating, but some scholars distinguish between the fallow year in Exodus 23:10-11; the sabbatical year in Leviticus 25:1-7, 18-22; and the *shemittah* year in Deuteronomy 15:1-11. For a thorough treatment, see John Sietze Bergsma, *The Jubilee from Leviticus to Qumran: A History of Interpretation* (Boston: Brill, 2007), 6.

163 "What applies to the Sabbatical Year applies equally to the Jubilee." Contained in the Halakic midrash to Leviticus. Jacob Neusner, *Sifra: Aharé mot, Qedoshim, Emor, Behar, and Behuqotai* (Tampa, FL: University of South Florida, 1988) 308-312, *Behar* 3:2. Also, Fred Skolnik, ed., *Encyclopaedia Judaica* (Woodbridge, CT: MacMillan Reference, 2007), volume 17, 623-630.

164 Jubilee was one of myriad juridical measures meant to foster social justice. Prohibition of usury and hoarding of collateral, tithing, prompt payments, and the rights to gleaning were also important. *Catechism*, 2449.

165 Even into our own day. Interestingly, the command from Leviticus 25:10 is inscribed on the U.S. Liberty Bell: "And thou shalt proclaim liberty in the Land for all its

This sums up well the message of Jesus: forgiveness, restoration, and liberty in the kingdom of God. At the beginning of his public ministry, Jesus stood in the synagogue and
read from Isaiah 61:1-2:

> "The Spirit of the Lord is upon me, because he has
> anointed me to preach good news to the poor. He has
> sent me to *proclaim release to the captives* and *recovering of sight*
> to the blind, to *set at liberty* those who are oppressed, to
> *proclaim the acceptable year of the Lord*." . . . And he began
> to say to them, "Today this scripture has been fulfilled in
> your hearing" (Luke 4:18-21).

The passage he read from Isaiah is a Jubilee declaration.
Jesus announces the purpose of his coming when he began his
ministry in that synagogue. Now, as his preaching ministry
is coming to a close with the Olivet Discourse, Jesus predicts that as the new High Priest "he will send out his angels
with a loud trumpet call." The Jubilee of forgiveness, restoration, and liberty will reach full force when he re-gathers his
Church after the upheaval of the Great Tribulation.

Why is this promise so important? *Because in the entire history of Israel, no Jubilee had ever actually been declared.*[166] Only
the High Priest could inaugurate it with the trumpet blast
and the sending of the messengers throughout Israel. The
priestly class had never found it financially advantageous
to declare it. This institutional injustice was the source of

---

inhabitants."Also Leviticus 25:8-17, 23-55.

166 Josephus, *Antiquities of the Jews*, 3:280ff. Also, *Sifra* 8:2 cited in Skolnik, ed., *Encyclopaedia Judaica*, volume 17, 623-630. Also, Nehemiah 5:1-13. But the *shemittah* did not
require the High Priest's proclamation, and so was observed after the return from exile
and into the second temple period. See Josephus, *Antiquities of the Jews*, 11:338; 14:202.
Also Nehemiah 10:31; 1 Maccabees 6:49-54.

intense resentment among common Jews, and the minor prophets railed against it repeatedly.[167] By the time of Jesus, some rabbis had gone so far as to teach a Jubilee announcement would not be appropriate: that the Jubilee *should not* be declared![168]

Jesus is the New High Priest. In contrast to the temple authorities—upon whom he has declared the sevenfold woes—he will make sure that the Jubilee trumpet blast sounds.[169] And his messengers will go not only to the land of Israel. The message will be sent "from one end of heaven to the other." He will declare the Jubilee forgiveness of sins, the Jubilee restoration into the family of God, the Jubilee liberty that only God's grace provides to all humanity.

How hopeful! Jesus' message does not end with the destruction of Jerusalem and its temple. Much had to be said about the false messiahs who were to appear. Much had to be said about the tribulation, the apostasy, the wickedness, and the destruction that was to come. The very survival of early Christianity depended on these warnings. But Jesus refuses to end on a sour note. He returns to a familiar

---

167 This was a source of conflict between priest and Essene, and also a reason why the zealots burned the debt and slave records when they killed the high priest. The Dead Sea Scrolls speak of the high priest, "the Wicked Priest, who . . . deserted God and betrayed the laws for the sake of riches . . . who will accumulate riches and loot from plundering the peoples. . . . Their loot will fall into the hands of the army of Kittim [Rome]" Florentino Garcia Martinez, ed., trans. W.G. Watson, *The Dead Sea Scrolls Translated: The Qumran Texts in English* (Boston: Brill, 1997), Pesher Habakkuk: 1QpHab 8-9. Also Margaret Barker, *The Time is Fulfilled: Jesus and the Jubilee, Scottish Journal of Theology,* 53:1 (Cambridge: Cambridge University Press, 2000), 22-32.

168 This is according to the *halakhah*. Maimonides later agreed in Mishneh Torah 10:1,8-10,15-16. Cited in Geoffry Wigoder, ed., *The New Standard Jewish Encyclopedia,* (New York: Encyclopedia Publishing Company, 1992), 818.

169 Isaiah, as we might expect from his Jubilee theme already noted, predicts this, "in that day a great trumpet will be blown, and those who were lost in the land of Assyria and those who were driven out to the land of Egypt will come and worship the LORD on the holy mountain at Jerusalem" (Isa. 27:13).

Old Testament theme: After tribulation there is always a re-
newed outpouring of God's grace and love. Jesus would not
have his followers doubt that the end to his story would be
filled with grace. He will gather his chosen people from the
four winds and renew them in the great Jubilee. That is his
parting promise. Coupled with the climax of the chiasm—
the preaching of the gospel—the young Church will have
plenty to sustain it through tribulation and displacement.

A B C D E F G H I J K L M Z M' L' K' J' I' H' G' F' E' D' C' B' A'
This generation (24:32-34)
*"From the fig tree learn its lesson: as soon as its branch becomes
tender and puts forth its leaves, you know that summer is near.
So also, when you see all these things, you know that he is near,
at the very gates. Truly, I say to you, this generation will not
pass away till all these things take place."*

We have arrived at the end of the inclusio. But first, two sen-
tences in segment A' emphasize the timeliness of the signs
Jesus has just enumerated. The signs are like a budding fig
tree. People in the ancient world knew that the fig tree did
not waste any time between its budding and its fruiting.[170]
Just so, the signs that the disciples will observe will assure
them that they are the "generation of the fig tree." The destruction of the temple is at hand, though it might look as
though Jerusalem is invincible. The signs they will be looking for include false messiahs, wars, famines, earthquakes,
tribulation, apostasy, gospel proclamation, and the Roman

---

170 Pliny, *Naturalis Historia: Natural History*, trans. John F. Healy (Penguin Classics, 1991),
5:18, "Wonderful is the haste of this fruit, one in all things hastening to maturity by
the art of nature."

army within Judea.

For upward of forty years after, the apostles must have looked at the advent of spring in a new light. Every budding fig tree must have reminded them of this discourse. As the signs started to unfold, they must have watched knowingly. But it would also have given urgent impetus to their proclamation of the gospel: the climax of Jesus' message in the chiasm and the only sign over which they had any control. They could—and they did—preach the gospel throughout the Roman world. Then, Jerusalem's temple would fall and the world as they knew it would end.

With Jesus' repetition of "this generation," this inclusio comes to an end. Jesus has delivered his warnings and predictions about Jerusalem's temple, and forty years later they proved right. If you understand who Jesus really is, then you understand how he could accomplish this impossible feat. Chrysostom made this point:

> Not only did [Christ] predict and foretell the destruction of the temple but he also prophesied during his life many other things which were going to come to pass a long time afterwards. Let us, then, bring these predictions into the open. If you see that he . . . tells the truth in all things and that this prediction has been fulfilled . . . [then] let us have no more of your impudence and stubbornness in matters which are clearer than the light of the sun.[171]

If you cling to the idea that Jesus was merely a good teacher, or perhaps even a charlatan, then there is no viable

---

171 St. John Chrysostom, *Against the Jews, in Discourses against Judaizing Christians*, trans. Paul W. Harkins, The Fathers of the Church, vol. 68 (Washington: Catholic University of America Press, 1979) Homily 5, 2:1.

explanation for his accuracy. So, Chrysostom calls it "impudence and stubbornness." Jesus' disciples bet their lives that he was correct. Their bet paid off for eternity.

THREE

The Close of the Age: Jesus Answers the Second Question in Matthew

Jesus has finished his first answer, and now segues into his second. In doing so, he highlights a theme that has been running below the surface of the entire first answer: the instability of the world and all creation.

For all its faults, our Western culture was built upon the foundation of Christianity, and it seems to me to be tremendously powerful and stable even now. I hope that it may long survive. The Jews of Jerusalem had likewise built a great civilization centered on the worship of God in his temple. What could be more stable than that? Perhaps we would say, "Only the very earth itself."

Jesus responds to this thinking with a promise: "Heaven and earth will pass away, but my words will not pass away" (Matt. 24:35). To sharpen the theme to a point: *The truth of Jesus is more stable and sure than any other reality.*

With their eyes, the disciples see the massive stones that make up the temple. With their ears, they hear the fleeting sound of Christ's words. Do they trust their eyes, or the Word of God? Many times they are not in agreement. Which is more permanent? Which is more stable? This sums up rather nicely the challenge to every follower of Christ.

This contrast also underpins the entire discourse. Segment

I, for example, warns that political stability will evaporate into war, societal structures will fail due to famine, and even the ground itself will be unstable. Nothing we believe to be stable will be sure. Yet, in the midst of all this, the climax of the chiasm assures us that the word of Christ will prevail—"this gospel of the kingdom will be preached throughout the whole world." Of course, that is precisely why the gospel *must* be preached with such urgency. God's truth is the only thing that will survive the ultimate collapse of all we believe to be stable.

That is the paradox of reality: What we see and touch is temporary. That which is permanent masquerades as the most tentative and ephemeral of realities: a word. It is only a breath, a fleeting meaning caught in the mind. But what makes this word so permanent is its source. Even though the name of that source sounds like a mere whisper—*YHWH*—this permanent word finds its wellspring in the Word, the eternal meaning and source of reality itself.[172]

That is the choice Jesus is laying before his disciples. Follow my word and what you build will endure for eternity. Follow your own senses to build a "permanent" temporal structure of any kind, and what you build will not last. Only following Christ leads to permanent greatness.[173]

That is the same choice Jesus lays before us today. We build houses and businesses and institutions and monuments because they seem to be more stable and permanent than our decaying bodies. We pray for just government, sufficient resources, good weather, fair treatment, and family loyalty. But

---

172 Notice that even God's name is different from the abrasive names of false gods such as Molech or Baal. Pope Benedict XVI has asked us to be respectful of the name of God, and thus avoid using it in liturgy. I use it just this once to illustrate this point.

173 St. Augustine wrote, "He will not be a great man who thinks it much that wood and stone should fall and mortals die." Lapide, *The Great Commentary*, Matthew 24:2.

when these things falter or disappear from our lives, we need to return to these words of Jesus. They will never fail us.

The end comes

Within the inclusio in the Olivet Discourse, Jesus gave the disciples information about the destruction of the temple, which would come in A.D. 70. In this, he answered the first of their two questions—*when will this be?*

But even while answering this question, Jesus showed he was less concerned about the "when" and more concerned about the survival of the truth in his Church. Without God's guidance, the persecutions, the false messiahs, and the Jewish-Roman War would have decimated the fledgling Church. The climax of his answer—and thus its most important point—was the disciples' responsibility to preach the gospel throughout the empire.

Now, Jesus leaves that topic to answer the second question the disciples asked: "What will be the sign of your coming and of the close of the age?" The "coming" in this context is not the middle coming in judgment that he predicts within the inclusio (first answer), but the final eschaton: the time at which Jesus will return in glory and the age will close into eternity.

How do we know that Jesus has gone from the first to the second question?

First, we know from the structure. The inclusio very clearly delineates the boundaries of the first question's answer. The end of the inclusio thus signals the beginning of the second answer.

Beyond that, we note that the essence of the answer changes dramatically. Jesus predicted that eight specific signs, which we examined, would precede the temple's destruction. All were fulfilled in the time leading up to the total destruction of the temple and its cult in A.D. 70. In contrast, the second answer offers a complete *lack* of any signs. The temple's destruction was guaranteed to be completed within a generation—forty years. In the second answer, Jesus proposes a timeline that will be long and indeterminate. The first answer's admonition kept returning to the rejection of false teachers and the preaching of the gospel. The second answer focuses on being productive and prepared for the Second Advent at all times, because it could happen at any time.

Even in English, the beginning of the second answer sounds like a change of topic. The paragraph starts with an abrupt phrase, "but of that day," signaling the end of one topic and the start of another. The days leading up to the temple's destruction were described in the plural—it would take a lengthy process to get to it. But the Second Advent is not a process—it is a "day," an "hour," a single event. It will happen suddenly and quickly, without sign or warning: think lightning.

What does Jesus mean when he says, "that day"? We need not look very far—only to the prior sentence.[174] That would be the most logical place to look for the antecedent: in the Thematic Segue. Jesus said, "Heaven and earth will pass away, but my words will not pass away. But of that day and hour no one knows." It seems obvious when we put the sentence down without the verse divisions: Jesus must be referring to the day when "heaven and earth pass away"—the end of the world.

Jesus did refer to the final eschaton once in his first answer, to contrast his Second Coming with the coming of the false messiahs that would precede the destruction of the

---

174 Brant Pitre, "Matthew 24" (paper presented at Applied Biblical Studies Conference, Steubenville, OH, July 2011). Also Brant James Pitre, *Jesus, the Tribulation, and the End of the Exile: Restoration Eschatology and the Origin of the Atonement*, (Grand Rapids, MI: Baker Academic, 2006).

temple. But now he is changing the subject, transitioning from the first answer to the second. He links them one to the other with the theme of stability and proceeds to discuss the Second Advent in detail. The final eschaton is the "day and hour" that will see the passing away of heaven and earth at the lightning-like "coming of the Son of man," and it is to be the subject of the second half of the discourse—from Matthew 24:35 to 25:46. Take some time now to read this passage, found in appendix A.

The structure

A skilled teacher, Jesus uses seven vignettes to drive home his message and make it easy to remember. These vignettes have a wealth of content. We can go back to them over and over and never cease to find a new lesson in them, but our task will be to glean just the basic thrust of the second answer. We have not lost sight of Russell's skepticism or Lewis's embarrassment. Now that Jesus really is talking about the end of the world, we can try to answer the skeptic's charge: Did Jesus wrongly anticipate the end of the world within his own generation?

For clarity, we will split the seven stories into two parts: six stories in the main answer and a final summary story. The structure of the main answer is what we might call a *parallel chiasm*, which we can represent like this: A-B, A-B, A-B, A-B-Z-B-A-B-Z. Each letter represents a topic, so you can see that the topics repeat over and over for emphasis. The climax, Z, comes only in the second half, where it appears twice. Jesus then tells the seventh story—the summary story—as a conclusion. This summary story, containing the familiar passage about the judgment of the sheep and the goats, repeats the climax three times: Z-B-Z-B-Z.

Here is what it looks like by topic.

Main Answer

	Story #
A *No one knows* the day or hour	1
B *Normal life* of Noah's contemporaries	1
A They *knew nothing*	1
B *Normal life* of one taken and one left	2
A Keep *awake*, you do *not know* the day	2
B *Normal life* of homeowner and thief	3
A Be *ready*, you do *not know* the hour	3
B *Normal life* of wise and wicked servants	4
Z Will come *unexpectedly* in *judgment*	4
B *Normal life* of foolish and wise bridesmaids	5
A Keep *awake*, you do *not know* the day or hour	5
B *Normal life* of two good servants and one lazy servant	6
Z *Judgment*	6

Summary Story

Z Son of Man in *judgment* of sheep	7
B *Normal life* of righteous	7
Z *Judgment* of goats	7
B *Normal life* of wicked	7
Z *Judgment* of both	7

Topic A: No one knows, so be alert

The topic of each segment A is the same: *No one knows the day or hour of the final eschaton.* This is the longest passage we have in which Jesus teaches about the Second Advent, and in it Jesus returns five times to this topic—no one knows the time of the end; in fact, no one *can* know it. Remember this the next time someone claims to have found a hidden date somewhere in the Bible. The hour of Christ's return is unknowable.

In the last three occurrences of segment A, Jesus adds an admonition: Since we cannot know when, the faithful Christian must always remain alert. The final eschaton could come at any time, so we must always be ready for it.

So, we see that Jesus does answer the second question presented to him. But, as with the first answer, his concerns are not identical to those of his disciples. They want a date and time. Instead, Jesus urges them always to be ready. As we will see, though, he does give them a couple of hints about timing—enough to prove Russell wrong.

Topic B: Normal life

Each of the six B segments in the main answer contains a story, and each of the stories revolves around the same topic: Life will be *normal* until the time when suddenly the end bursts upon us. This is in stark contrast to the eight signs that preceded the middle coming of A.D. 70.

The six B segments make clear why some will *not* be ready for the Second Advent. Each one speaks to the ordinariness of life prior to the Second Coming. They describe a variety of people involved in a wide range of commonplace activities. In each story, Jesus describes one type of person who would be ready for him when he returned, and another type of person who would not be ready.

If life seems to be ordinary, then all the more reason to remain alert to Christ's message. As St. Augustine wrote, "The last day lies hid, that all days may be watched."[175]

The Church has applied this lesson in every generation. You and I may not live to experience the final end of the world. But in our death, we will experience every bit of "the end" that we can handle. So, since we do not know

---

175 St. Augustine, in Lapide, *The Great Commentary.* Matthew 25:14.

when our own end will come, we must always be ready for it. *Memento mori,* as medieval monks used to remind one another—"Remember your death." Life may be completely normal, and then the fatal auto accident occurs. Or, maybe it is a heart attack. Or, maybe it is choking on a blueberry at a family reunion (as once happened to me).[176] We must never let the ordinariness of life lull us into believing that the end cannot happen before we finish our next meal.

Topic Z: Judgment

The climax appears five times: twice in the main answer, and then three more times in the summary story. This mirrors the five times that segment A appears in the main answer. It is the climax that explains why it is so important to be ready during our everyday lives. At the Second Coming of Jesus Christ, all will be judged. The climax constitutes the main thrust of Jesus' answer: We must be ready, because we will be judged at a time we cannot predict.

The first two times the topic of judgment is raised, segment Z comprises only one sentence. But in the summary story, the judgment occupies center stage. The dialogue alternates between B—normal life—and Z, the final judgment. In the summary story, Jesus has already come, and so it is a look back at normal life interspersed with the judgment that life has earned.

AB AB AB ABZBABZ

No one knows (24:36)

"But of that day and hour no one knows, not even the angels of heaven, nor the Son, but the Father only."

---

176 This would have been the end for me if not for my sister's quick and effective intervention. Thank you, Sandy.

There is no wiggle room in these words—no man, no angel, nor even the Blessed Mother knows the time of Christ's coming. Jesus even includes himself in this category, which should remove all doubt about whether *we* could somehow figure it out.

This, of course, raises a question. How can Jesus not know what the Father knows, since he is consubstantial with the Father? After all, Jesus did say, "All that the Father has is mine" (John 16:15) and "I and the Father are one" (John 10:30). This question goes to the heart of the Incarnation and the Trinity. But, rather than try to plumb the Christological conundrum raised by Jesus' words—for which Catholic tradition supplies more than one orthodox interpretation—we will take a practical approach. Namely: Why would Jesus make this statement in the first place?

Jesus does this to show us the only way to be successfully human. His lesson, in stating the proposition as he does, is that we must choose obedience and faith over independence and certitude. An obedient disciple does not try to discern what his master claims he doesn't need to know.

We can go a step further. In this statement it is clear that Jesus did not even show a desire to know the day or hour. If you *could* know—if you had the chance to be the first human to have this knowledge, would you want it? The disciples certainly desired this knowledge—that was the question that began this entire discourse. But, if we want to imitate Jesus, the answer should be "no." We should not seek knowledge that Christ tells us is strictly the Father's business.

This illustrates why Jesus stands as the New Adam. The first Adam was created from the overflow of Trinitarian love; but rather than respond to that love with grateful obedience, Adam turned away from it towards self-love, eating of the forbidden tree of knowledge. Seduced by the envious

serpent, and yielding to his prideful rebellion, Adam sought
to *know*, when God wanted him to wait and *trust*.

Adam wanted to know so that he could be "like God" (Gen.
3:4), master of right and wrong, in control of his own destiny.
We have already seen that this is an issue for the disciples as well.
They desire answers about the timing of the final eschaton in
order to get one step ahead of the game; to be in a position to
control the events following the destruction of the temple.

In contrast, Jesus takes the self-love embedded in the human race ever since Adam and through his Incarnation and
Passion turns it into *self-sacrificing* love—thereby crucifying
both the desire for inappropriate knowledge and the craving
for control. His attitude toward knowledge in this answer
to the disciples is an outgrowth of that love. Jesus displays
disregard for knowledge of the time of the end. In so doing,
he shows us how to entrust our own future to his Father.
As St. Paul wrote, "Let the same mind be in you that was in
Christ Jesus, who . . . emptied himself . . . humbled himself,
and became obedient" (Phil. 2:5-8).

Many are not willing to follow this example. Like Adam,
many throughout history have desired a knowledge that is
not intended for them. Those that seek to determine the
hour of the final eschaton are—perhaps unconsciously—
trying to gain independence from God. If a man were to
know the hour of judgment, then he could seek to plan his
life without any dependence on God.[177] Of course, some
have attempted to predict the time of the end in order to
spur their peers to greater ardor. It is not my purpose to
judge another man's motives or holiness. But the plain fact

---

177   Faith is the opposite of this attitude. "The obedience of faith is to be given to God...
an obedience by which man commits his whole self freely to God, offering the full
submission of intellect and will." *Dogmatic Constitution on Divine Revelation, Dei Verbum*:
Second Vatican Council (Vatican, 1965), 5.

is that despite Jesus' admonition, Christians continue to seek knowledge of the time of Christ's coming.

How much clearer could Jesus have been? No man knows the day or hour, and there's no way we can figure it out; no hidden scriptural key; no heavenly or earthly sign to watch for. As Christians, we must follow our master's example and not seek, or even desire, to know what is the province of God alone.

AB AB AB ABZBABZ

Just like the flood (24:37–39)

"As were the days of Noah, so will be the coming of the Son of man. For as in those days before the flood they were eating and drinking, marrying and giving in marriage, until the day when Noah entered the ark, and they did not know until the flood came and swept them all away, so will be the coming of the Son of man."

The first illustration that Jesus uses to help us understand his point centers on Noah and the flood. God commanded Noah to build an ark, but the rest of the world was "eating and drinking, marrying and giving in marriage." Average people were oblivious to the coming judgment, living their everyday lives right up until the flood.

Likewise, the Second Coming will come even as life progresses normally; even as people are looking ahead hopefully to the future. (Few people would bother getting married if they believed the world was about to end.) In sharp contrast to the signs of Jesus' middle coming in A.D. 70—including social and political upheavals that the disciples could recognize—the normalcy of life and the world around us will provide no hint of the Second Advent.

We should not assume that Jesus is saying that there will

be no chance for repentance. Noah preached to his neighbors for many years as he built the ark, and we can hope that the Church will be preaching, teaching, and calling us back to the Lord until the very end. But God shut the door of the ark before the floods began.

AB AB AB ABZBABZ

One taken, one left (24:40-41)

"Then two men will be in the field; one is taken and one is left. Two women will be grinding at the mill; one is taken and one is left."

After Jesus warns a second time that the time of the end is unknowable, he tells another story to illustrate the point. In each of his examples, two people are at work, with one taken and one left.

Dispensationalist preachers have widely and famously abused these two verses.[178] For our purposes, let us just remind ourselves of two important points. First, no one will be "left behind" for anything. There are two people living their normal lives, and one is taken and one is left. Dispensationalists have added the word "behind," which does not appear in the passage, to make these verses support their extrabiblical notion of a "rapture of true believers."

Second, in the context of the passage there is no room for anything after being taken or being left other than the final judgment. There is no room for an imaginary seven-year tribulation or a utopian thousand-year messianic kingdom centered in Jerusalem. The context of the passage makes clear that the final judgment is the *next event* after being taken and being left.

---

178 They are ubiquitous on the radio, convincing others that our generation will not die before the "Rapture" of true believers. For full exploration, see my book *Rapture*, 5-41ff.

This one sentence about the taking and leaving of friends likely shocks the disciples. Jesus tells them that prepared and unprepared people will be comingled in society. At this point they may still believe that Christ's kingdom will be geographical and political—in which case, kingdom people will be segregated from unbelievers. But, here it is clear that people loyal to the kingdom will be interspersed as friends and coworkers of those who are not. They will be separated only when Christ returns. As St. Ambrose said, "No one may trust to good society merely because he lives among the righteous. That judgment will separate father from son, wife from husband, brother from brother."[179]

This kingdom of Christ is certainly no mere political entity. Rather, "the kingdom of heaven is like leaven which a woman took and hid in three measures of flour, till it was all leavened" (Matt. 13:33). Christ will rule in the hearts of the faithful. Those few faithful will be interspersed in society. Through his loyal subjects, Christ will bring about the transformation of civil society.

We should note one more interesting point: This single event—the Second Coming—will occur at two different times of day. In Luke we read,

"I tell you, in that night there will be two in one bed; one will be taken and the other left. There will be two women grinding together; one will be taken and the other left" (17:34–35).

Two people are sleeping at night when the end comes. Yet, at the same moment that lightning strikes—when the end arrives—two women will be working at midday. This is fur-

---

179 St. Ambrose, quoted in Lapide, *The Great Commentary*, Luke 27:35.

ther evidence that Christ is speaking of a worldwide end—the final one. Only by including the entire world could both midday and nighttime be included in the same instantaneous event. The entire world will meet its end at the same moment, and all will be caught in whatever state they are in.

AB AB AB ABZBABZ

A thief in the night (24:42–44)

"Watch therefore, for you do not know on what day your Lord is coming. But know this, that if the householder had known in what part of the night the thief was coming, he would have watched and would not have let his house be broken into. Therefore you also must be ready; for the Son of man is coming at an hour you do not expect."

Jesus warns a third time that we must be ready, since we cannot know the day of his return. But, he does give a little hint of when it might occur: when we do not expect it! This leads into an interesting analogy in this third story: Jesus likens his coming to that of a thief. Every property owner knows that he is susceptible to theft. Because he cannot pinpoint the exact moment it might happen, it is essential that he is on guard and vigilant at all times.

Although it may seem odd to liken Christ to a thief, we find this analogy used elsewhere in the New Testament by Peter, Paul, and John.[180] The analogy actually addresses a common misconception. Some believe that if only we knew when Christ was returning, it would make us more devout and faithful. But this is not true. If we know when the thief is coming,

---

180 1 Thessalonians 5:2–4, 2 Peter 3:10, Revelation 3:3, 16:15. The first two uses of "thief" speak of Christ's Second Coming, while the last two speak of middle comings.

we are alert only *at that time*. Think about it: Knowing the day of the Second Advent would make us even more lackadaisical than we already tend to be. "If, now that we know *not* the end, we are careless, what should we do if we knew it? We should keep on our wickedness even unto the end."[181]

Luke makes this connection explicit. "Be on guard so that your hearts are not weighed down with dissipation and drunkenness and the worries of this life, and that day does not catch you unexpectedly, like a trap" (Luke 21:34-35). Whether a trap or a thief, the point is the same: We must be continually on our guard because we don't know when.

AB AB AB ABZBABZ

A tale of two servants (24:45-49)

"Who then is the faithful and wise servant, whom his master has set over his household, to give them their food at the proper time? Blessed is that servant whom his master when he comes will find so doing. Truly, I say to you, he will set him over all his possessions. But if that wicked servant says to himself, 'My master is delayed,' and begins to beat his fellow servants, and eats and drinks with the drunken...."

For a fourth time Jesus reminds his disciples they cannot know the time of the end. To illustrate this, he tells the story of two servants put in charge of their master's household. The faithful and wise servant conscientiously tends those under his care.[182] He knows "the delay . . . is a time

---

181 Theophylact of Ohrid, quoted in Aquinas, *Catena Aurea*, Mark 13:32-36.

182 Jesus deals only with judgment, not rewards, in this parable. But his use of the word "wise" would have made the disciples remember Daniel 12:3. "And those who are wise shall shine like the brightness of the firmament; and those who turn many to righteousness, like the stars for ever and ever."

of repentance."[183] The wicked servant, however, takes advantage of his underlings because the master is absent longer than expected. He uses the delay as an opportunity for self-indulgence.

This delay of the master is actually another small hint. Jesus has just taught that his Second Coming will be at an unexpected time, and now he says that it will be *later than expected*. Skeptics like Russell seem to have missed this part. Far from predicting an imminent return in glory, Jesus specifically states that he will be "absent" for longer than expected. As a result of that delay, some will start to doubt the return of Christ at all and start to abuse their positions of responsibility.

This story has traditionally been understood as applying primarily to the leadership of Christ's Church. It certainly does have a message for them, enumerating the two major clerical temptations of imperiousness and luxury. (St. Boniface, who led the conversion of Germany, wrote of the latter, "Formerly priests of gold celebrated in chalices of wood; now priests of wood celebrate in chalices of gold.")[184] But, since we know there is also a "domestic church" in every Christian home, this message also speaks to every father and mother. Parents also are tempted to imperiousness and selfish luxury. Parents have "underlings" for whom they will someday give an account. Sometimes the end of childhood seems to be delayed forever, but parents don't get the chance to raise their children a second time. The advice of Jesus: Be wise and faithful parents.

---

183 St. Hilary of Poitiers, quoted in Lapide, *The Great Commentary*, Matthew 25:1-30.

184 Lapide, *The Great Commentary*, Matthew 25:46.

AB AB AB ABZBABZ

Judgment expanded (24:50-51)

*"[T]he master of that servant will come on a day
when he does not expect him and at an hour he does not know,
and will punish him, and put him with the hypocrites;
there men will weep and gnash their teeth."*

At this point, for the first time in this answer, Jesus reaches his thematic climax—explaining *why* it is so important to be ready for the master's return. We must be ready because when he comes again there will be *judgment*.

Peter, who had listened intently to these words of Jesus, would, in his first epistle, focus on the same two vices of leadership that Jesus enumerated, reminding his readers to avoid them and so to win a just reward at the judgment.

> I exhort the elders among you to tend the flock of God that is in your charge . . . not for *sordid gain* but eagerly. *Do not lord it over* those in your charge, but be examples to the flock. And when the chief shepherd appears, you will win the crown of glory that never fades away (1 Pet. 5:1-4).

Interestingly, in this first mention of the judgment, Jesus addresses the fate only of the wicked servant. He is to be punished with the hypocrites. We tend to think of a hypocrite as someone who says one thing publicly and does another in private. But Jesus and his listeners were steeped in the literature of the Proverbs, where the hypocrite is the man who is lazy about his spiritual obligations while being fastidiously diligent in his pleasures.

The leaders of the Church who are overly concerned with their own authority or their own comfort are no different. And these words apply equally to any parent, as head of the domestic church. Think of the father who can arise without an alarm to go golfing but has trouble getting up for Mass with his children. Note the mother who can tirelessly shop at the mall but has trouble finding time to really listen to her child. Or, the couples who plan their family vacations in minute detail but never think about how they and their children will spend eternity. These are the hypocrites of Proverbs.

AB AB AB ABZBABZ

Maidens wise and foolish (25:1-12)

"Then the kingdom of heaven shall be compared to ten maidens who took their lamps and went to meet the bridegroom. Five of them were foolish, and five were wise. For when the foolish took their lamps, they took no oil with them; but the wise took flasks of oil with their lamps. As the bridegroom was delayed, they all slumbered and slept. But at midnight there was a cry, 'Behold, the bridegroom! Come out to meet him.' Then all those maidens rose and trimmed their lamps. And the foolish said to the wise, 'Give us some of your oil, for our lamps are going out.' But the wise replied, 'Perhaps there will not be enough for us and for you; go rather to the dealers and buy for yourselves.' And while they went to buy, the bridegroom came, and those who were ready went in with him to the marriage feast; and the door was shut. Afterward the other maidens came also, saying, 'Lord, lord, open to us.' But he replied, 'Truly, I say to you, I do not know you.'"

Imagine a gaggle of ten bridesmaids all in a room—pitch black, as any ancient wedding feast would have been without lamps. Five maidens are wise enough to bring enough oil, while five foolish ones are not. This parable reminds us again that the good and bad will be mixed until the final judgment.[185]

The maidens are waiting for the marriage supper, a symbol of our entrance into eternal beatitude. The marriage supper of the Lamb "is the putting on of immortality, and the joining together of corruption and incorruption in a new union."[186]

Although some of the Fathers of the Church understood this parable as referring to consecrated virgins,[187] others disagreed.[188] Those wrote that the lessons here are applicable to all of us: We must not only be alert when the Bridegroom comes—the wise will ready by preparing for it *ahead of time*.

The Fathers have interpreted the lamp as a symbol of our faith, with the accumulated oil symbolizing our good works.[189] This understanding coincides with Jesus' own words elsewhere. In the Sermon on the Mount Jesus declared, "Let your light so shine before men, that they may see your good works and give glory to your Father who is in heaven" (Matt. 5:16).

---

185   St. Gregory of Nyssa and St. Jerome. In addition, St. John Chrysostom noted that it is possible to have some oil, but not enough. All cited in Aquinas, *Catena Aurea*, Matthew 25:1-13.

186   St. Hillary of Poitiers, quoted in Aquinas, *Catena Aurea*, Matthew 25:1-13.

187   "Maidens" can be translated as "virgins." John Chrysostom, *Homily 78* on Matthew 25 in Schaff, *Nicene and Post-Nicene Fathers*, vol. 10. Also, Theophylact of Ohrid, St. Augustine, and St. Gregory, in Lapide, *The Great Commentary*, Matthew 25:1-12.

188   St. Jerome acknowledged that many believed maidens referred only to the consecrated, but wrote, "I think the meaning to be different, and that the parable has reference not to virgins only but to the whole human race." Quoted in Aquinas, *Catena Aurea*, Matthew 25:1-13. In fact, it has been aptly pointed out that the lessons of this one parable sum up the entire message of Jesus throughout all of Matthew. See Karl Paul Donfried, *"The Allegory of the Ten Virgins as a Summary of Matthean Theology," Journal of Biblical Literature* 93, 3 (1974), 415ff.

189   St. John Chrysostom, *Homily 78* on Matthew 25, in Schaff, *Nicene and Post-Nicene Fathers*, vol. 10. Also, Origen and Auctor Operis Imperfecti (an anonymous author of antiquity often quoted), both cited in Lapide, *The Great Commentary*, Matthew 25:1-12. Also, St. Jerome, St. Hillary of Poitiers, both cited in Aquinas, *Catena Aurea*, Matthew 25:1-13. Also, St. Thomas Aquinas, *Catena Aurea*, Matthew 25:14-30. Also, "Charity, which is the flame of the lamps, that is, of souls, is nourished by good works, as by oil." Lapide, *The Great Commentary*, Matthew 25:1-30.

St. James put the same thought into different words when he wrote that "faith by itself, if it has no works, is dead" (James 2:17). We must have faith (the lamp) and works (the oil) together if we're to make charity (the light of God's life) shine abundantly. "Faith is an entirely free gift that God makes to man . . . but he also asks for a radical choice . . . Words are not enough, deeds are required."[190]

When the foolish maidens awake from sleep, they realize their plight. So, they attempt to borrow the oil of the wise. It may seem selfish of the wise to refuse, but it is true to reality. No one can borrow the good works of another. "In the day of judgment no one's virtues will be able to give any assistance to other men's faults."[191] Judgment will be individual.

When the Bridegroom arrives, the time for good works is finished. "After the judgment there is no more place for prayers or merits."[192] Reformation can be too little as well as too late. "There will be no profit in the confession, forced by necessity, of him who never once voluntarily confessed."[193] The words of the judge here, "I do not know you" (Matt. 25:12) were anticipated in the Sermon on the Mount: "I never knew you" (Matt. 7:23).

AB AB AB ABZBABZ

Keep awake! (25:13)

"Watch therefore, for you know neither the day nor the hour."

---

190 *Catechism*, 162 and 546.

191 St. Jerome, quoted in Lapide, *The Great Commentary*, Matthew 25:9. St. John Chrysostom agreed, cited in Aquinas, *Catena Aurea*, Matthew 25:1-13.

192 St. Augustine, quoted in Aquinas, *Catena Aurea*, Matthew 25:1-13.

193 Auctor Operis Imperfecti, quoted in Lapide, *The Great Commentary*, Matthew 25:1-12.

At the end of the story of the maidens, Jesus returns for the fifth and final time to his initial point: No one knows when the end will come, so do not follow the example of the sleepy, foolish maidens. Instead, stay awake and watch.

Remaining in the state of constant watchfulness can be difficult. There might even be the temptation to view one's own Christian fervor as inferior to those who seem to know so much about the end times. But St. Augustine would have none of that. He wrote, "A person does not seem to me to be in error when he knows that he does not know something, but when he thinks that he knows what he does not know."[194]

In this story, Jesus alludes a third time to the timing of his Second Advent. Like the master in the previous story, the bridegroom is "delayed." The Fathers understood the delay to be so long that the sleep of the maidens signifies their death.[195] The delayed Second Coming precipitates the problem of the foolish maidens (their lack of oil) and reminds us that only those who are watchful, prepared, diligent, and faithful to the end will be rewarded. There is no way to know when the Second Advent will occur, so we must always be ready with our oil, practicing good works. For most of us, the Christian life is a marathon, not a dash. The foolish maidens were prepared for the latter, while the wise ran the former.

St. Gregory had this to say: "Since ye know not the day of judgment, prepare the light of good works. For he who has guaranteed pardon to the penitent has not promised tomorrow to the sinner."[196]

---

194 St. Augustine, quoted in Aquinas, *Catena Aurea*, Matthew 25:25-27.

195 St. Jerome, St. Augustine, St. Gregory of Nyssa; all cited in Aquinas, *Catena Aurea*, Matthew 25:1-13.

196 St. Gregory, quoted in Lapide, *The Great Commentary*, Matthew 25:13.

AB AB AB ABZBABz

No cookie-cutter servants (25:14-18)

"For it will be as when a man going on a journey called his
servants and entrusted to them his property; to one he gave five
talents, to another two, to another one, to each according to his ability.
Then he went away. He who had received the five talents went
at once and traded with them; and he made five talents more.
So also, he who had the two talents made two talents more.
But he who had received the one talent went and dug in the
ground and hid his master's money."

The final story of the main answer shows that our situation may be slightly more complex than we have thought. In all the previous stories, people have been taken or left—included or excluded from the eternal kingdom. The criterion for judgment has been their behavior during their normal lives. But it is not quite that simple. This last story before the summary story is about three servants who are entrusted with varying talents to invest while their master is gone.

All the servants receive at least one talent (talents were literally a measurement of money), which are the natural endowments we are given by God.[197] "There is no man who can say with truth, 'I have not received a single talent. There is nothing of which I must give an account.'"[198] We will each be evaluated based on what we are given, not upon what we wish we had been given, or what we were given in comparison to another.

The first two servants are not given the same number of talents, but they do not let any comparison bother them.

---

197 These natural endowments are obviously undeserved but must not be confused with initial, or primary, grace. That is another topic entirely; it can be investigated under "grace" in the *Catechism*.

198 St. Gregory, quoted in Lapide, *The Great Commentary*, Matthew 25:14-30.

They understand that with added talent comes added responsibility.[199] The servant who is given only one talent, on the other hand, turns bitter. He is convinced that the master is fundamentally unfair.

Having lost faith in his master's goodness, he never puts to good use the talent that he does have. He does not seem to understand that talents, few or many, must be utilized for others. So, "when you see one who has the power . . . of benefiting souls, hiding this power, though he may have a certain religiousness of life, doubt not of such an one that he has received one talent and hides it in the earth."[200]

Remember how the Fathers understood the oil of the maidens to be their good works? St. John Chrysostom taught that the lesson of the three servants develops further the lesson of the maidens.[201] We must utilize the talents God gives us, doing good works (oil) in the context of our faith (lamp), in order to please the master (with light). Some have less to work with, while others are blessed with more. Yet, each one will be judged based only on what God has given—on the disposition of the will toward serving rather than just the increase gained.

The Lord does not regard so much the greatness of the gain as the goodwill and the desire. And it is possible that he who receives two talents, by trading diligently with them, may merit more than he who receives five and uses them in a lukewarm manner.[202]

---

199 "Therefore should everyone be humble concerning his talents in proportion as he sees himself tied up with a greater responsibility." St. Gregory of Nyssa, quoted in Aquinas, *Catena Aurea*, Matthew 25:14-30.

200 St. Gregory of Nyssa, quoted in Aquinas, *Catena Aurea*, Matthew 25:14-30.

201 St. John Chrysostom, cited in Aquinas, *Catena Aurea*, Matthew 25:14-30.

202 St. Jerome (Origen agreed), quoted in Aquinas, *Catena Aurea*, Matthew 25:22-23.

Notice also the freedom the master grants to each servant.[203] He does not micromanage them with harassing letters while he is away. They are free agents entrusted with a noble task, just as you and I are. If the penurious servant wishes to bury his talent, the master will not override his choice. God is patient with us.[204] But every servant will eventually be judged.

AB AB AB ABZBABZ

Rewards will vary (25:19-30)

"Now after a long time the master of those servants came and settled accounts with them. And he who had received the five talents came forward, bringing five talents more, saying, 'Master, you delivered to me five talents; here I have made five talents more.' His master said to him, 'Well done, good and faithful servant; you have been faithful over a little, I will set you over much; enter into the joy of your master.' And he also who had the two talents came forward, saying, 'Master, you delivered to me two talents; here I have made two talents more.' His master said to him, 'Well done, good and faithful servant; you have been faithful over a little, I will set you over much; enter into the joy of your master.' He also who had received the one talent came forward, saying, 'Master, I knew you to be a hard man, reaping where you did not sow, and gathering where you did not winnow; so I was afraid, and I went and hid your talent in the ground. Here you have what is yours.' But his master answered him, 'You wicked and slothful servant! You knew that I reap where I have not sowed, and gather where I have not winnowed? Then you ought to have invested my money with the bankers, and at my coming I should have received what was my own with interest.

---

203 St. Thomas Aquinas, *Catena Aurea*, Matthew 25:14-30.
204 St. John Chrysostom, cited in Aquinas, *Catena Aurea*, Matthew 25:14-30.

So take the talent from him, and give it to him who has the ten talents. For to every one who has will more be given, and he will have abundance; but from him who has not, even what he has will be taken away. And cast the worthless servant into the outer darkness; there men will weep and gnash their teeth.'"

The judgment—Z once more—completes the story seamlessly. We learn that the judgment will not be some cursory look at our earthly attitudes towards the vaguely spiritual. Nor will it be some heavenly pop quiz administered at the gates of heaven to determine our level of spiritual knowledge. Our judgment will be based upon the use of our individual gifts. Talents given must be used for others.[205] Each servant is rewarded, based on performance and disposition of will. St. Paul picked up on the teaching of this parable when he wrote, "we urge you also not to accept the grace of God in vain" (2 Cor. 6:11).

The one talent that the wicked servant did possess was taken from him and given to a productive servant. (Notice that the master did not keep it for himself.) This little insight gives us a snapshot of the interpersonal relationships in hell. The man with the gift of making others laugh will no longer do that in hell; that gift will be taken from him. The woman with the gift of empathy will not be able to help others in hell. No one will want to help *anyone* else. All of God's gifts, meant to be given to others, will be withdrawn. Paul knew well that this lays an obligation upon those whom God has endowed with talents. He declared, "Necessity is laid upon me. Woe to me if I do not preach the gospel!" (1 Cor. 9:16).[206]

---

205 St. Bede wrote, "To tie up money in a napkin, is to hide our gifts under the idleness of a lifeless torpor." Quoted in Aquinas, *Catena Aurea*, Luke 19:11-27.

206 St. Gregory of Nyssa wrote, "[How] shall I endure His presence, to whom, in return for the work I have undertaken, I bring no gain of souls, or almost none?" Quoted in Lapide, *The Great Commentary*, Luke 19:13.

For a fourth time, Jesus gives a hint about the timing of the final eschaton: The master returned "after a long time." Jesus is repeatedly preparing his followers for a long wait before his return. It is so consistently clear that Jesus did not expect the Second Advent to occur quickly—does it take willful blindness to miss it?

ZBZBZ

The general judgment (25:31-36)

"When the Son of man comes in his glory, and all the angels with him, then he will sit on his glorious throne. Before him will be gathered all the nations, and he will separate them one from another as a shepherd separates the sheep from the goats, and he will place the sheep at his right hand, but the goats at the left. Then the King will say to those at his right hand, 'Come, O blessed of my Father, inherit the kingdom prepared for you from the foundation of the world; for I was hungry and you gave me food, I was thirsty and you gave me drink, I was a stranger and you welcomed me, I was naked and you clothed me, I was sick and you visited me, I was in prison and you came to me.'"

We have completed the main answer to the disciples' second question. All that remains in Matthew is the summary story, though it is actually much more than that. Up to this point, Jesus has been telling parables—fictional stories that give insight into life and judgment. In this last story, Jesus actually *describes* the general judgment.[207] In so doing, he drives home the climax of the entire second answer. The

---

207 St. John Chrysostom, "Christ does not accordingly say of this as of the others, 'The kingdom of heaven is like,' but shows of Himself by direct revelation, saying, 'When the Son of man shall come in his majesty.'" Quoted in Aquinas, *Catena Aurea*, Matthew 25:31-45.

disciples want to know the "when" of the end of the world. Christ wants them to understand the "who, what, why, and how" of the approaching judgment. If they can understand those, the "when" becomes unimportant. He has repeatedly taught that "when" would be delayed and its suddenness would catch many unprepared.

The first thing we notice is that Christ will judge in majesty. No humble carpenter here—Christ will empty heaven of angels in order to accompany him in his glory.[208] This is the "King of kings and Lord of lords" described in the Apocalypse.[209] He will judge all: emperors, kings, princes, philosophers, and pontiffs.

One interesting interpretation is that these angels are actually the human leadership of Christ's Church, as St. Augustine believed.[210] If so, the disciples probably need this foretaste of the future: In a few short days they will see Christ arrested, interrogated, ridiculed, rejected, flogged, and crucified. They will hide in an upper room in abject fear. But that is not the end of the story. The final judgment Jesus is describing will write the last sentence.[211]

The first act of judgment is to separate all people into two groups. This is a big change! Earlier in this passage, we heard of two women grinding flour together when Christ returns. We heard of maidens awaiting the bridegroom, both wise and foolish intermingled. We heard about the two good servants working alongside the penurious servant while the master was gone. But now is the moment of truth.

---

208 *Catechism*, 331. Also, Hebrews 1:14. Also, Lapide, *The Great Commentary*, Matthew 25:31-45.

209 "On his robe and on his thigh he has a name inscribed, King of kings and Lord of lords" (Rev. 19:16).

210 St. Augustine understood the angels as "messengers" that are righteous men sitting with Christ in judgment. Augustine, cited in Aquinas, *Catena Aurea*, Matthew 25:31-45.

211 St. Jerome, cited in Lapide, *The Great Commentary*, Matthew 25:31-45.

Once the two groups are segregated, their differences come to light. "Then shall sinners see their sins, and the righteous shall see clearly to what end the seeds of righteousness in them have led."[212]

This is an echo of an event in the Old Testament. When Israel entered the Promised Land, Moses commanded the people to separate into two groups. Half of the tribes stood on a hill to the left of the Levites, and the other half of the tribes stood on a hill to the right. With the Levites leading, they shouted the curses that accompanied the breaking of the Law. Then, they enumerated blessing on those who obeyed God's Law (Deut. 27:11-14). It was a warning to Israel about keeping the Law of Moses. In the judgment scene before us, the type is fulfilled. Christ stands as the ultimate Priest, separating the people for blessing and for cursing.

Sheep and goats symbolize the two separated groups. The sheep will be blessed for all eternity, while the goats will be accursed. The sheep have followed in the footsteps of him who was "led as a sheep to the slaughter."[213] They are characterized by simplicity, innocence, and humility.[214] In contrast, goats in ancient time were thought of as quarrelsome, lascivious, and fierce.[215] So, the characters of the people within the two groups are substantively different: righteous versus wicked.

The sheep discover that God will not remain in anyone's debt. "He who is kind to the poor lends to the LORD, and he will repay him for his deed" (Prov. 19:17). The sheep are

---

212 Origen, quoted in Aquinas, *Catena Aurea*, Matthew 25:31-45.

213 The Suffering Servant passage (Isaiah 53:7) is applied to Jesus in Acts 8:32.

214 *Catechism*, 544.

215 The two animals are contrasted thus by St. Jerome, St. Thomas, and Origen, cited in Aquinas, *Catena Aurea*, Matthew 25:31-45. Also Lapide, *The Great Commentary*, Matthew 25:31-45.

rewarded for their kindness to Christ when he was in need. What the sheep did for him does not seem extraordinary, merely simple kindness. For example, they did not attempt to free Christ from prison, but they did visit him.[216] This work of mercy is richly—even fantastically—rewarded. Paul was aware of the imbalance when he wrote,

> I consider that the sufferings of this present time are not worth comparing with the glory that is to be revealed to us. . . . No eye has seen, nor ear heard, nor the heart of man conceived, what God has prepared for those who love him.[217]

The sheep are told that they will inherit an entire kingdom, one that was "prepared for you from the foundation of the world." Remember this declaration the next time you admire a beautiful sunset or marvel at a mountain view. Your reward with God in heaven was prepared for you before the first sunset existed. The purpose of physical creation is to create a stage on which to accomplish our salvation.

And we will *inherit* God's kingdom. This concept of inheriting is prominent in Psalm 37, which King David wrote as an older man. In it, he contemplates the problem of evil people and their apparent prosperity. He questions how it is possible to claim that there is justice in a world where good people suffer and evil people do not.[218] Jesus answers the question by extending our vision beyond the present to the final judgment that ushers in eternity. As Pope Benedict has

---

216 St. John Chrysostom, cited in Aquinas, *Catena Aurea*, Matthew 25:31-45.

217 Romans 8:18 and 1 Corinthians 2:9. Also Rabanus Maurus Magnentius, cited in Aquinas, *Catena Aurea*, Matthew 25:31-45.

218 Psalm 37:9, 11, 22, 29, 34. Matthew 5:5, "Blessed are the meek, for they will inherit the earth" can also be considered a reflection of Psalm 37.

written, only a final judgment—*in the body*, after death, by an all-knowing God—satisfies the demands of ultimate justice.[219] Chrysostom and Origen made the same point.[220] The book of Wisdom illustrates that this has been the answer to David's question for much of salvation history.

> Then the righteous man will stand with great confidence in the presence of those who . . . made light of his labors. [The unrighteous] will be amazed at his unexpected salvation. They will speak to one another in repentance. . . . "This is the man whom we once held in derision! . . . It was we who strayed from the way of truth. . . . What has our arrogance profited us?" (Wis. 5:1-8).

The language that Jesus borrows from Psalm 37 ("inheriting") reminds us that the final judgment corrects the wrongs leftover from our life on earth. Of course, this inheritance language also implies kinship—the status of a son. Although the earlier parables in Matthew liken us to servants, in reality we are *children* of God. As Paul wrote,

> For you did not receive the spirit of slavery . . . [but] the spirit of sonship. . . . We are children of God, and if children, then heirs, heirs of God and fellow heirs with Christ provided we suffer with him in order that we may also be glorified with him (Rom. 8:15-17).

---

219 "A world which has to create its own justice is a world without hope . . . there can be no justice without a resurrection of the dead." Pope Benedict XVI, *Spe Salvi: Saved in Hope* (Vatican: Encyclical Letter, 2007), 42.

220 Origen wrote, "Come, that in *whatever they are behind they may make it up* when they are more perfectly united to Christ." And St. John Chrysostom wrote, "Observe that He says not 'Receive,' but possess, or inherit, as *due to you* from of old." Both quoted in Aquinas, Catena Aurea, Matthew 25:31-45.

Truly, our kinship status is a gift—made possible by the Passion of our Lord.[221]

Paul's language corresponds to this judgment scene. The sheep are the children of God who inherit, but that inheritance is earned by their responsible actions as sons. They fed, refreshed, welcomed, clothed, and visited Christ when he needed them. They responded to the grace of God with righteous action.[222]

ZBZBZ

Everyday life of righteous sheep (25:37–40)

"Then the righteous will answer him, 'Lord, when did we see thee hungry and feed thee, or thirsty and give thee drink? And when did we see thee a stranger and welcome thee, or naked and clothe thee? And when did we see thee sick or in prison and visit thee?' And the King will answer them, 'Truly, I say to you, as you did it to one of the least of these my brethren, you did it to me.'"

Frankly, Christ's blessing confuses the sheep! When did they encounter Jesus? And who would dare to refuse help to Christ if they did?

In their questions, the sheep exhibit humility that contrasts to the lazy servant entrusted with one talent in the last story.[223] Remember his reaction upon the return of his master? He blamed his master for his laziness! He had a rebellious

---

221 Scott Hahn, *Kinship by Covenant: A Canonical Approach to the Fulfillment of God's Saving Promises* (New Haven, CT: Anchor Yale Bible Library, 2009).

222 As St. Augustine wrote, "Ye go into My Kingdom, not because ye have not sinned, but because ye have redeemed your sins by alms." Quoted in Lapide, *The Great Commentary*, Matthew 25:35–36.

223 Origen, "It is from humility that they declare themselves unworthy of any praise for their good deeds, not that they are forgetful of what they have done." Quoted in Aquinas, *Catena Aurea*, Matthew 25:31–45.

inner attitude that manifested itself in pride rather than humility, selfishness rather than selflessness, disobedience rather than obedience.

The sheep learn that help given "to the least of these" is actually counted as help given to Christ. "The least of these" almost certainly refers to the apostles and those that followed them—men devoted completely to the spreading of the gospel. Jesus has just spoken of the Great Tribulation in the first answer. Christians would be in need merely because they were loyal Christians.[224] There have always been those in need because of their faith.[225]

But, this statement may be applied to everyone in need. The *Catechism* teaches us that, "Jesus identifies himself with the poor of every kind and makes active love toward them the condition for entering his kingdom."[226] Because Christians make up the mystical body of Christ, helping our brothers and sisters when they are in need really is helping Christ.[227]

While they awaited the Second Advent, the sheep have been faithfully practicing the works of mercy. Jesus praises the sheep for helping Christian brothers who were in need of food, water, welcome, clothing, care, and encouragement while in prison. Although the Judge mentions only the corporal works, the Fathers taught that Jesus did not intend to exclude the spiritual works of mercy.[228] Remember the par-

---

224 They "will arrest you and persecute you; they will hand you over to synagogues and prisons" (Luke 21:12).

225 St. Francis believed that his friars, by begging, gave Christians an opportunity to become the sheep of this passage. Francis, cited in Lapide, *The Great Commentary*, Matthew 25:31-45.

226 *Catechism*, 544.

227 "God has so composed the body . . . that the members may have the same care for one another. If one member suffers, all suffer together. . . . You are the body of Christ and individually members of it." 1 Corinthians 12:24-27. Also, *Catechism*, 669.

228 St. Jerome, "He seems to me not to speak of the poor generally, but of the poor in spirit." Also, Origen, "It is not one kind of righteousness only that is rewarded, as

able of the ten maidens. Works of mercy are the oil contained in the lamp of faith. The faith and works together produce the supernatural charity that brings light to the world. These combined allow the maidens entrance into the wedding feast.

When we perform works of mercy—putting oil into our lamps—*we will be changed.* God uses the act of almsgiving to transform our souls. Augustine wrote, "It is written, as water extinguishes fire, so doth alms extinguish sin."[229] And, "whoever gives alms worthily for his sins, first begins with himself."[230] It is true that "the soul which is rich in mercy can never be overwhelmed with heavy troubles of the mind," because "uselessly will sins accuse him."[231]

St. Francis believed that aiding the poor helped to rid the soul of pride, the Achilles' heel of so many. That may be why St. Augustine taught that "some men cannot be saved without almsgiving."[232]

The liturgy teaches this same lesson. Christ gives himself to us in the Eucharist, and we are to give ourselves to others.[233] "The Eucharist commits us to the poor. To receive in truth the Body and Blood of Christ given up for us, we must recognize Christ in the poorest, his brethren."[234] Chrysostom chided those Christians who received Eucharist but showed no mercy to others. You have tasted the Blood of the Lord, yet you . . . dishonor this table when you do not judge worthy of sharing your food someone judged worthy to take part in

---

many think. In whatsoever matters any one does Christ's commands, he gives Christ meat and drink." Also Remigius of Auxerre, Rabanus Maurus Magnentius. Quoted in Aquinas, *Catena Aurea*, Matthew 25:31–45.

229 St. Augustine, quoted in Lapide, *The Great Commentary*, Matthew 25:46.
230 St. Augustine, quoted in Aquinas, *Catena Aurea*, Matthew 25:46.
231 St. John Chrysostom, quoted in Lapide, *The Great Commentary*, Matthew 25:31–45.
232 St. Augustine, quoted in Aquinas, *Catena Aurea*, Matthew 25:46.
233 This touches on the teaching of "mystagogy" in the Fathers: the mystery of Christ accessed in the sacraments and living through us in our daily lives.
234 *Catechism*, 1397.

this meal. . . . God freed you from all your sins and invited you here, but you have not become more merciful.[235]

As you might have guessed, this concept is also rooted in the Old Testament. Daniel urged the proud king of Babylon to save himself through works of mercy: "Break off your sins by practicing righteousness, and your iniquities by showing mercy to the oppressed" (Dan. 4:27). The practice of mercy and righteousness would displace the iniquity in the king's soul. David expresses it a little differently. "It is well with the man who deals generously.... He has given to the poor; his righteousness endures forever" (Ps. 112:5-9).

Forever! That is exactly what the blessing on the righteous sheep entails: blessedness forever in heaven.

ZBZBZ

Reward of the Goats (25:41-43)

"Then he will say to those at his left hand, 'Depart from me, you cursed, into the eternal fire prepared for the devil and his angels; for I was hungry and you gave me no food, I was thirsty and you gave me no drink, I was a stranger and you did not welcome me, naked and you did not clothe me, sick and in prison and you did not visit me.'"

Not everyone is a sheep. Those on Christ's left—the wicked goats—are to be punished for all eternity.[236] This is not a popular concept today. "How could a loving God punish *forever?*" Do not be fooled into thinking that this is a sophisticated objection that finds its source in enlightened modernism. The human challenge to God on the basis of mercy

---

235 St. John Chrysostom, quoted in *Catechism* 1397.

236 St. Jerome, "Let the thoughtful reader observe that punishments are eternal." Quoted in Aquinas, *Catena Aurea*, Matthew 25:46.

has been around since Christ spoke these words. Since Jesus himself said the punishment was forever, St. Gregory of Nyssa answered the challenge thus: "While they go out of the way to prove God merciful, they are not afraid to charge him with fraud."[237]

We sometimes forget that this forever place of judgment was not even created for mankind. Hell was created for Satan and the other fallen angels. Only by attaching themselves to the works of Satan do the wicked goats make hell their own eternal destiny.

> God did not, as far as in Him lay, create men to perdition, but sinners yoke themselves to the devil, so that as they that are saved are made equal to the holy angels, they that perish are made equal with the devil's angels.[238]

As St. John wrote, "He who does not love abides in death" (1 John 3:14). Hell is the logical result of the choices the goats make against love. In life, they refused to perform works of mercy. Just as the performance of these works changes us for the better, so the refusal to show mercy will stiffen our souls in rebellion.[239]

This command of Christ to the goats—"Depart!"—has a fascinating background in the Old Testament. Once a year, on the Day of Atonement (Yom Kippur), the Israelites would gather as the high priest made collective atonement for their sins. Then, the nation would begin the year anew, striving to live as God's holy people. One of the ceremonies

---

237 St. Gregory of Nyssa, quoted in Aquinas, *Catena Aurea*, Matthew 25:46. Also, St. Augustine cited there.
238 Origen, quoted in Aquinas, *Catena Aurea*, Matthew 25:31-45.
239 This is the logical conclusion of the phrase in the Our Father, ". . . forgive us our debts, as we also have forgiven our debtors . . ." Matthew 6:9-13.

that cleansed Israel of sin involved sending a goat away from the camp to carry the nation's sins with it into the wilderness. This emissary goat was sent to *"Azazel"* (cf. Lev. 16).

What, or who, was this *Azazel* to whom the sins were carried? It is complex, but by examining other Hebrew literature written between the time of Moses and Jesus, the picture is clear enough.[240] *Azazel* was most likely a rugged cliff in the wilderness over which the emissary goat was cast.[241] This cliff went by this name because it was believed that a fallen angel named *Azazel* was imprisoned there.[242] The name *Azazel* means "arrogant toward God."[243] (According to Origen, *Azazel* is actually another name for Satan.[244])

It is not hard to understand why Israel's sins were sent to a fallen angel whose name meant "arrogant toward God." The prophets repeatedly labeled Israel as arrogant, proud, presumptuous, and stubborn.[245] These attitudes lead to a refusal to obey God's Law. In their arrogance and pride, the Israelites disobeyed God year after year, from one *Yom*

---

240 Though not canonical, 1 Enoch is a good source. The first 36 chapters were written around 300 BC. The Ethiopic Orthodox consider the book canonical. See R.H. Charles, *The Book of Enoch, or 1 Enoch* (Oxford: Parker, 1912).

241 1 Enoch 10:4. Also, Rashi the great medieval Jewish grammarian, in Rashi, *Metsudah Chumash Rashi*, ed., Nachum Y. Kornfeld, Abraham B. Walzer, and Avrohom Davis (Jersey City, NJ: KTAV Publishing House, 1997), vol. 3, Leviticus 16. Also, the Talmud called "Azazel . . . the hardest of mountains" and mentions the rebellious "Uza and Azazel." Isidore Epstein, ed., *The Babylonian Talmud* (London: Soncino Press, 1948), yoma 67b.

242 1 Enoch 8:1-3. Also, R.H. Charles, *1 Enoch, The Apocrypha and Pseudepigrapha of the Old Testament*, vol. 1, (Berkeley, CA: Apocryphile Press, 2004), commentary on Enoch 10:4.

243 Many angel names end in –el, which is a name of God. There is Gabri-el, and Micha-el, and Rapha-el; and also Azaz-el. *Azaz* means strength, but for a fallen angel would have a negative connotation, such as impudence or arrogance to God. See Nathaniel Schmidt, *Original Language of the Parables of Enoch*, in *Old Testament and Semitic Studies in Memory of William Rainey Harper*, vol. 2, ed., Robert Francis Harper, Francis Brown, and George Foot Moore (Chicago, IL: University of Chicago Press, 1908), 343–345.

244 "The serpent . . . in the Hebrew language is named Azazel." Origen, *Contra Celsum*, 6:43; in Roberts, *Ante-Nicene Fathers*, vol. 4. See also John Granger Cook, *The Interpretation of the Old Testament in Greco-Roman Paganism*, (Tubingen, Germany: Paul Mohr Verlag, 2004), 299.

245 For example, Nehemiah 9:16, 29.

Kippur to the next. It was fitting to command "Depart!" to an emissary goat laden with prideful sins; to cast it into the prison of the angelic author of pride and arrogance.

How is this type fulfilled in the final judgment? The new high priest—Christ—commands "Depart!" to the goats. He sends away those wicked people who refused to show mercy when he was in need. They closed their souls to love and obedience. They are sent—like the emissary goat of *Yom Kippur*—to spend eternity with imprisoned, prideful demons who also refused to obey God.

ZBZBZ

Everyday life of the goats (25:44-45)

"Then they also will answer, 'Lord, when did we see thee hungry or thirsty or a stranger or naked or sick or in prison, and did not minister to thee?' Then he will answer them, 'Truly, I say to you, as you did it not to one of the least of these, you did it not to me.'"

Of course, we all knew this statement exchange was coming. Just as the righteous sheep helped Jesus by helping those people around them, the wicked goats *refused to help* those they encountered in life. They had the opportunity—we all do—but they refused: Their sin was one of omission.

Why refuse to help? Assorted authors have used different words to describe the goats' motivation. Chrysostom used the terms avarice and covetousness; Theophylact of Ohrid, lack of compassion; Francis of Assisi, pride.[246] When we combine

---

246 St. John Chrysostom, "Avarice blinds men to all these considerations." Quoted in Aquinas, *Catena Aurea*, Matthew 25:31-45. Also, St. John Chrysostom: "They were held back by covetousness." Theophylact of Ohrid, "They who are without compassion are devils." St. Francis rebuked his friar for pride as already related. All quoted in Lapide, *The Great Commentary*, Matthew 25:31-45.

all the images before us, it gives us a composite picture that agrees with them all. The goat was a stubborn, lascivious creature. *Azazel* was an arrogant spirit who refused to obey God. Israel was proud and stubbornly self-serving. There we have it. The goats refuse to help the needy because of the goats' pride, born of an arrogant desire to satisfy their own desires. Their egocentric choices leave no room for the compassion God enjoins. God instructs us to be compassionate as he is compassionate. Those who refuse to obey find that "hell embraces . . . those who deny [the instruction of God]."[247]

Unfortunately, our culture has embraced egocentric, disobedient pride as a virtue.

> The characteristic of the modern age is that men concentrate on themselves and what they can and want to do. This and this alone is what life is about. No outside source can guide, command, or coerce us. Man is autonomous. . . . He does not make himself into what he "ought" to be. The word "ought" has no meaning [in the modern age].[248]

Arrogant pride and selfish envy caused *Azazel* to fall from heaven. Those humans that embrace his stubborn arrogance will initially feel that they can change course whenever they so desire; subsequently, they do not want to change course; then they cannot change course; and finally they are in hell with *Azazel*—where arrogance and envy are the norm—forever.[249]

---

247 St. Cyprian (Tascius Caecilius Cyprianus) quoted in Lapide, *The Great Commentary*, Matthew 25:45. Cyprian understood. He was a wealthy man that gave much of his wealth away after his baptism in the third century.

248 James V. Schall, S.J., "The Point of Christianity," *Crisis Magazine*, July 18, 2012.

249 St. Gregory of Nyssa, "How shall [those in heaven] pray for [those in hell] when any change from their wickedness is no longer possible?" Quoted in Aquinas, *Catena Aurea*, Matthew 25:46.

ZBZBZ

Two eternal rewards (25:46)

*"And they will go away into eternal punishment,
but the righteous into eternal life."*

Jesus arranged his narrative in this summary story on the last
judgment in an interesting order. First, he dealt with the righteous sheep, and only then with the wicked goats. But in this
final statement, he reverses that order. By placing the sheep
last, he is able to end his discourse with the reward of the
righteous.[250] This ends the Olivet Discourse, which had begun with the promise of destruction, on an encouraging note.

When we reflect on Christ's entire answer to the disciples' second question, it becomes clear that his desire to
"incite us to good" is not limited to this last statement but
underlies all the stories.[251] The five climaxes, contained in
each segment Z, drive home the reality of the impending
final judgment. How we live our lives while waiting for the
Second Advent, contained in every segment B, emerges as
vitally important. We are, moment by moment, making the
bed in which we will lie for all of eternity.

His disciples would have known that the Old Testament
taught that "the wicked [shall] . . . not see the majesty of
the LORD" (Isa. 26:10). But the righteous sheep will. Jesus
promised, "Blessed are the pure in heart, for they shall see
God" (Matt. 5:8). "That which the Lord spoke to His servant Moses, 'I am that I am,' this we shall contemplate when
we shall live in eternity."[252]

---

250 Salvation and reward are the natural work of Christ, and judgment his duty. Origen,
quoted in Aquinas, *Catena Aurea*, Matthew 25:46. Also *Catechism*, 679.
251 Origen, quoted in Aquinas, *Catena Aurea*, Matthew 25:46.
252 John 17:3 is contained in this quote of St. Thomas, *Catena Aurea*, Matthew 25:46.

What will it mean to contemplate God forever? Many have tried to describe this future, but it surpasses our abilities. Eternal life means "the receiving of all health, all strength, all honor, all glory, all pleasure, all joy, and everything that is good."[253] We will find that "heaven is the ultimate end and fulfillment of the deepest human longings, the state of supreme, definitive happiness."[254] We will "rejoice in the delights of the immortality bestowed upon us in the company of . . . the friends of God."[255] We will revel in knowing that there will be no death—nor even a lingering whiff of decay—to separate us from our unadulterated joy.

God will be the center of our focus. We will "see the divine essence with an intuitive vision, and even face to face, without the mediation of any creature."[256] We will be "like God for ever, for [we shall] 'see him as he is,' face to face:"[257] This is *theosis,* the divinization of man: not in the evil sense associated with wizards and shamans, nor in the implausible, independent godhood suggested by the Mormons, but divination as the Fathers of the Church meant it. We shall be *like God* because he will have adopted us as his family. Endowed with incorruptibility, clarity, agility, and subtlety, the saints in heaven are like God.[258] Of course, we can never be God by nature. But, our eternal state is to become as close to that

---

253 Lapide, *The Great Commentary,* Matthew 25:46.

254 *Catechism,* 1024.

255 St. Cyprian, *The Letters of St. Cyprian of Carthage: Ancient Christian Writers,* vol. 3, ed., G. W. Clarke (Mahwah, NJ: Paulist Press, 1986) letter 58, 10:1, 67. We will share "in the good things of God that utterly surpasses the understanding of the human mind."*Dogmatic Constitution on the Catholic Faith, Dei Filius:* First Vatican Council (Vatican, 1890), 2:4.

256 Pope Benedict XII, *Benedictus Deus:* On the Beatific Vision of God (Vatican: Constitution, 1336), 1.

257 *Catechism,* 1023, quoting 1 John 3:2.

258 These four attributes are enunciated in 1 Cor. 15:42-44. They mean we will be immune to pain and decay, luminous with joy, endowed with physical mobility, and have complete spiritual control of our bodies.

as is possible. Through the Son—who is God by nature—we become partakers of the divine nature.[259]

Summing up

Having examined the Olivet Discourse in Matthew, I trust you can now understand that arguments against Christ's reliability based on his end-times predictions are a dead letter. Russell, Schweitzer, Lewis, and our college student believed that Jesus expected the final eschaton within that generation. Each of them made decisions about their Christian commitments based on this misunderstanding. They failed to see what Church tradition has long taught: There is more than one question and answer contained in the Olivet Discourse.

The first question of the disciples was about the temple's destruction. In his first answer, Jesus describes the fall of the temple by utilizing language and imagery common to the Old Testament. The skeptics and embarrassed Christians fail to note this context and what it signifies. Likewise, they ignore the structure of the passage—both the inclusio and the chiasm—and so wrongly apply the first answer to the second question. This leads them to the wrong conclusion: that Jesus was wrong about the end of the world. But, by carefully examining each idea, we see that it is the skeptics who are mistaken. Christ remains a trustworthy witness of reality.

The second question of the disciples *did* involve the end of the world and the Second Advent. Before Jesus begins to answer that question, there is a "hard break" in his answer. The inclusio ends, and the topic clearly shifts. In his answer to that question, Jesus repeatedly emphasizes that his Second

---

259 St. Athanasius, St. Clement of Alexandria, and St. Irenaeus all emphasized divinization. "The Son of God became man so as to deify us in Himself," Quoted in J.N.D. Kelly, *Early Christian Doctrines,* 5th edition (London: A.C. Black, 1977), 378.

Advent will not come as quickly as his disciples assumed. There will be a long wait—a delay. Jesus promises that he *will* return in glory, but it will *not* be soon.

Could the disciples have imagined that it might be 2,000 years and counting? Perhaps not. But we should have no illusions. Jesus knew it would extend much farther than his disciples imagined, perhaps even farther than we can imagine. But it will come—it will most assuredly come. In the meantime, Jesus predicted a delay so lengthy that many Christians would face their own end, their own personal judgment at their death long before the Second Advent. The story of the ten maidens addresses this issue. St. Jerome wrote, "That which shall happen to all in the Day of Judgment is fulfilled in each at the day of death."[260]

Perhaps it is now apparent why the Second Coming—like death itself—will come unannounced. Otherwise, people would worry about their eternal state only in the moments immediately prior to their judgment. As Chrysostom said, "If men knew surely when they were to die, at that time only would they seek to repent."[261]

It might serve modern man well to keep in mind the words of the ancient desert mystic, St. Anthony.

> When we awake out of sleep, let us be in doubt whether we shall see the evening. When we lay us down to rest, let us not be confident that we shall come to the light of another day. Thus we shall not offend, nor be carried away by vain desires. Neither shall we be angry, nor covet to lay up earthly treasures.[262]

---

260 St. Jerome, Commentary on Joel, quoted in Lapide, *The Great Commentary*, Matthew 24:42.
261 Lapide, *The Great Commentary*, Matthew 25:42.
262 St. Athanasius, quoted by Lapide, *The Great Commentary*, Matthew 25:42.

FOUR

A Kingdom in Your Midst: Jesus Elaborates in Luke

There are five accounts in the synoptic Gospels that cover the apocalyptic material we are examining. We have completed three of them. The Olivet Discourse in Matthew is the longest of the parallel passages. Mark's single account is shorter than Matthew's; in fact, everything we learned in Matthew 24-25 can be applied to Mark 13. Luke, on the other hand, is more complex, splitting the material into three accounts. Luke 21 is strikingly similar in setting and structure to both Matthew and Mark. As we examined Matthew, we alluded to Mark 13 and Luke 21, so we will not examine them independently. Luke 17 and 19, however, contain additional material embedded into dramatically different settings.

Matthew records a private discussion about the end of the temple and the end of the world. The four closest disciples ask the questions, and it is likely that no one outside the Twelve were privy to the details that Jesus related. Luke 17 and 19 record a very different scene. In these two accounts, his opponents publicly confront Jesus. His answer is heard by friend and enemy alike.

Does a different audience cause you to change your tone and emphasis? Do you confide to your closest friend about things you would never share with a cantankerous neighbor? Does hostility make you guard your words? Your audience can make all the difference in the world!

There is, undoubtedly, overlap material between Luke 17/19 and Matthew 23-25, and some scholars think that they are actually all the same event, edited and placed into different settings by the Gospel authors. But, there is no reason to assume that Jesus told his stories only once. Like any popular teacher, he probably used the same stories with slight variations on different occasions, thereby emphasizing different lessons. This was especially important in a culture that did not record every word on video and post it on YouTube. Repetition aided recall.

So, we must avoid reflexively telescoping all five passages into one historical event. The Fathers certainly believed these were three different events in five passages, not one conversation transposed into different settings.[263] The most straightforward approach is to take Luke's decision as trustworthy: There were three different conversations. Matthew, Mark, and Luke 21 concern the private discussion we examined already. Then, there are two more conversations—undeniably similar but also strikingly different. Fortuitously, this canonical approach to these passages also makes them more understandable. And, the important differences in Luke will help us to garner new insights into what Jesus taught about the end of the world.

Luke 19

Since it consists of a single parable, we will discuss Luke 19 first. (The text of the parable maybe found in Appendix B.) The scene in Luke takes place a couple of days before the discourse in Matthew. On his journey to Jerusalem and the Passion, Jesus meets Zacchaeus the tax collector in Jericho.

---

263 St. John Chrysostom, Euthymius, and Jansen; all cited in Lapide, *The Great Commentary*, Matthew 25:14.

He is about seventeen miles east-northeast of Jerusalem. Jesus is speaking in a public forum. His enemies are criticizing him for associating with a social outcast—a turncoat tax collector.

Luke tells us exactly why this conversation occurred: Jesus' followers believe that the "kingdom of God is to appear immediately." In other words, they are expecting the final consummation—the reestablishment of David's throne—to arrive when Jesus reaches Jerusalem. They expect the end of the age—the end of the world—to occur not merely within a generation but in *a day or two*. They suppose that the final eschaton is truly imminent. Schweitzer would have fit right in.

If Jesus had ever wanted to propose an immediate end of the world, this is his golden opportunity. The atmosphere around him is filled with giddy anticipation. The final conflict in the temple has not yet occurred. You can almost hear the people urging: "Now! Declare that your glorious coronation is at hand!" The triumphal entry is about to take Jerusalem by storm, so why not strike while the iron is hot?

But, Jesus does the unexpected. He tells a parable that throws a wet blanket on the elation of his followers, specifically contradicting this false impression that the kingdom will appear soon.

The parable is similar to—and yet different from—the story of the talents in Matthew. We encounter again the servants who are given varying amounts to use for their overlord. The gifts they receive and then multiply are the basis for measuring their final reward. Yes, all we have is a result of divine grace, which enables our work to be supernaturally pleasing to God. Yet, at the same time, in our freedom we must cooperate with supernatural grace: Our wills must say yes. As St. Paul put it:

> But by the grace of God I am what I am, and his grace toward me was not in vain. On the contrary, I worked

harder than any of them, though it was not I, but the grace of God which is with me (1 Cor. 15:10).

There remain three key differences between Luke and Matthew. First, the servants are given something other than talents. Luke records the servants being given *mnas*, or *minas*. It took sixty *mnas* to make one talent. But the importance of this word lies in its Old Testament backdrop. When Belshazzar, king of Babylon, witnessed the disembodied handwriting on the wall of his palace, he called Daniel to interpret. The first two words on the wall were a repetition of the word *mana* (or *mene* or *mna*).[264] The word translates literally as "he numbered," but Daniel interpreted it as a decree of judgment on the ruling dynasty. "God has numbered the days of your kingdom and brought it to an end" (Dan. 5:26). So an aura of God's judgment attached to the word.

A second major difference: The overlord in Luke's account is not a "master" but a "nobleman," or royalty. He goes away to a "far country," which the Fathers understood to be heaven. Jesus will go there upon his Ascension and return at the Second Advent. So, "this part of the parable is about the Second Advent."[265]

However, the most important difference involves an entirely new group of people introduced into the parable. There are "citizens" who urge the nobleman not to return. They "hated him and sent an embassy after him, saying, 'We do not want this man to reign over us'" (v. 14). Clearly, we can understand why this would not be needed in a private discussion directed only at loyal disciples, as in Matthew. In this parable, Jesus is address-

---

264 Vowels were not originally written in Hebrew, so it can be tricky. For details see Lapide, *The Great Commentary*, Luke 19:13.

265 Euthymius. Also, St. Jerome, St. Augustine, St. Bede, Origen, and Theophylact of Ohrid. All quoted in Lapide, *The Great Commentary*, Luke 19:12-15, Matthew 25:1-30.

ing the rebellious Jewish leaders. They are the citizens. Many of them will shout, "We have no king but Caesar" (John 19:15). They will provoke the crowd to cry, "Crucify him!"

Upon his return, the nobleman deals first with his servants (as in Matthew). We are in for a treat, because we get a little taste of the afterlife. The two servants do not just get a pat on the back with a "Well done, lad!" from their king. They are given additional *authority* over cities. When we enter eternity, our service to God continues. And so, today, we have places that venerate saints as their special patrons: St. James in Spain, St. Dionysius in Paris, St. Ambrose in Milan, St. Boniface in Germany, and so on. God has put them into positions of spiritual authority in heaven. There is evidence of this veneration in the catacombs of Rome. Those saints that precede us into their particular judgment are rewarded with the power to work miracles in proportion to their past earthly faithfulness.

> They . . . constantly care for those whom they have left on earth. . . . In the glory of heaven the blessed continue joyfully to fulfill God's will in relation to other men. . . . Their intercession is their most exalted service to God's plan. We can and should ask them to intercede for us and for the whole world.[266]

Asking favors of these saints has always been an integral part of Christian belief and practice.

Then, the king turns his attention to the rebellious citizens. His words are chilling: "As for these enemies of mine, who did not want me to reign over them, bring them here and slay them before me" (v. 27). This is not the wishy-washy Jesus of Christian bedtime stories: This is the King of all cre-

---

266 *Catechism*, 1029, 2683.

ation come back in the final judgment. Now Luke's use of the word *mnas* rather than *talents* makes sense. This parable is a public warning of judgment on the ruling elite of Jerusalem.

It certainly can be applied to the judgment of A.D. 70 under the Romans. In that sense, the slaying recalls what the Babylonians did when they destroyed the first temple. They "slew the sons of [King] Zedekiah before his eyes, and put out the eyes of Zedekiah, and bound him in fetters, and took him to Babylon" (2 Kings 25:7). But the primary reference of the parable is to the final judgment also described in Matthew 25.

Luke and Matthew contain two similar stories with significant differences. They are told at different times, in different locations, to different audiences. In Luke, the *mnas* that the servants are given emphasizes judgment—the audience was not the close-knit group of disciples that it was in Matthew. In Luke, the "master" is a "nobleman." This allows for the introduction of a new group of people, the citizens that reject the nobleman. They reject the nobleman's authority, but the story ends with a day of reckoning—the final judgment. When Jesus told the parable in Luke, some of the rebellious citizens were listening.[267]

Luke 17

Only one passage remains, although chronologically Luke 17 occurs prior to the others we have examined. Jesus is in the process of traveling to Jerusalem, where Matthew 23-25 occurs. He has not yet gotten to Jericho where he will meet Zacchaeus in Luke 19.

You may recall that the Matthean passage contains two questions and two answers, and that the first answer is organized into a chiasm. This structure helped the ancients

---

267 Some of the Fathers taught that the servants were all Christians and the citizens were those that reject Christ.

to remember the passage, and it also helps us to be able to decipher its meaning. By looking at the corresponding segments, we can more easily understand difficult phrases, such as those about eagles and lightning. Likewise, Luke 17:20–37 forms a chiasm (the passage can be found in Appendix B):

A   Control asserted (17:20a)
  B   Kingdom's advent indiscernible (17:20b)
    C   Kingdom in your midst (17:21)
      D   Cannot secure the Messiah (17:22)
        E   Do not pursue (17:23)
          F   Day of the Son of Man (17:24)
            G   Suffering (17:25)
              H   Eating and drinking (17:26–27a)
                Z   Salvation and destruction (17:27b)
              H' Eating and drinking (17:28)
            G' Destruction (17:29)
          F' Day of the Son of Man (17:30)
        E' Do flee (17:31)
      D' Cannot secure life (17:32–33)
    C' Kingdom intermingled (17:34–35)
  B' Kingdom's advent indiscernible (17:37a)
A' Control denied (17:37b)

A B C D E F G H Z H' G' F' E' D' C' B' A'

Control asserted (17:20a)

"Being asked by the Pharisees when the kingdom of God was coming . . ."

As the scene opens, the Jewish authorities challenge Jesus about his message. For three years Jesus has been preaching the good news: The kingdom of God is coming! Yet, the

Romans are undoubtedly still in charge of Judea. David's reestablished kingdom is nowhere in sight. Jesus is on his way to Jerusalem, where he knows he will be rejected and crucified. Many of the religious authorities—primarily the Pharisees and Sadducees—will be seeking his death.

We might imagine this Pharisee questioning Jesus with a curl of the lip, fully intending to mock whatever answer Jesus gives.[268] (Perhaps I am too harsh, but I have no difficulty imagining Bertrand Russell himself asking this Pharisee's question.) Jesus probably left the Pharisee in bewilderment, for the answer he gives is carefully constructed and complex.

Notice that this is a public answer given to a hostile questioner; we should expect a public discourse with unbelievers to be different than an intimate conversation with disciples.[269] And indeed, compared with Matthew this discourse includes new information and leaves out other information. Even the climax of Luke changes due to the hostile audience that Jesus is addressing.

Using some imagination, we might recast the Pharisees' attitude toward Jesus in more modern terms:

"Jesus, we want you to know that we are Pharisees. Moreover, we are all members of a special Committee of the Sanhedrin for Evaluating Claims of a Kingdom—COTS-FECK for short. See the emblem embroidered on each of our tunics? But let's get to the point. It has come to our attention that you are claiming—entirely without official sanction—that the promised kingdom is upon us. As the duly appointed

268 Euthymius, "They asked Him when He would reign, as to deride Him, who appeared as one of low estate." Quoted in Lapide, *The Great Commentary*, Luke 17:20. Also, St. Cyril, "Pharisees derided Him." Quoted in Aquinas, *Catena Aurea*, Luke 17:21.
269 Earlier, Jesus had said to his disciples, "To you it has been given to know the secrets of the kingdom of heaven, but to them it has not been given. . . . This is why I speak to them in parables" (Matt. 13:11-15).

COTS-FECK authority, we must know when we can expect
to see any visible evidence of this kingdom. We will then vote
on it and refer our decision to the full Sanhedrin."

I hope my artistic license has helped make the Pharisees'
intention clear: control.[270] They are confronting Jesus in
their role as the recognized spiritual leaders of Jerusalem. If
Jesus is going to preach the "kingdom gospel" in *their* city,
he had better know that *they are in charge*. He is answerable
to them. They are in control of the religious situation in
Jerusalem, and they must verify his claims.

They want to know the *when* of the kingdom, which fits in
perfectly with our present investigation: Did Jesus believe his
glorious coronation and reign would occur within a generation?

A B C D E F G H Z H' G' F' E' D' C' B' A'

Kingdom's advent indiscernible (17:20b)

*"[H]e answered them, 'The kingdom of God is not
coming with signs to be observed.'"*

At first blush, Jesus' answer in segment B seems a bit odd. But
upon reflection, its purpose becomes clear. Jesus immediately
pops the Pharisees' pompous balloon by turning the conversation in another direction. He informs them that they want to
control the advent of something that they have already missed!
The kingdom of God came, but without the outward signs and
fanfare they expect. Instead, it came like a mustard seed sown in
the ground (Matt. 13:31). It came as a small, poor baby in a tiny,
insignificant village. But it is present and growing. You are so

---

270 Since the answer given to them in corresponding segment A' is identical to that given
to the disciples in Matthew, we can deduce that the disciples were after some semblance
of control as well.

busy with your committee work, says Jesus, with keeping control of everything, with protecting your own self-interest that you were unprepared for the kingdom when it came.

The unobservable nature of the kingdom helps to make sense of the disciples' question later in the chiasm's parallel segment B'. Toward the end of the dialogue they ask where all this will happen. The answer to the "where" is the same as the answer to the "when." The kingdom came—as it always comes—without observable signs, in places and times unforeseen by men, outside the realm of human control.

The message of segment B is simple. You cannot know where the kingdom is by looking for the kinds of political signposts you expect. It is already here in the person of Jesus Christ, and it will work its way through society like yeast through a bowl of dough, unseen to those who do not know where to look. The coming of the kingdom will always be unobservable by the typical indicators of this world.

A B C D E F G H Z H' G' F' E' D' C' B' A'

Kingdom in your midst (17:21)

"[N]or will they say, 'Lo, here it is!' or 'There!' for behold, the kingdom of God is in the midst of you."

Here, Jesus sounds like he is about to speak about the false messiahs, but he takes things in a different direction. Remember, he is addressing people who are basically accusing him of being a false prophet; so he finishes his sentence to the Pharisees by speaking what must have seemed like a riddle. It's not a question of when the kingdom will arrive. It is *already here* "in the midst of you," inaugurated by Jesus, who is standing right before you. Where the king is, there his kingdom is present. The kingdom of God has been—and will continue to be—"in the midst of them." It is within all those that accept it as "reigning in their hearts by faith."[271]

The kingdom of God on the whole is to live after the manner of the angels, when nothing of this world occupies our souls. We need no long time and no distant journey, for faith is near us, and after faith the divine life.[272]

Jesus doesn't need the approval of the religious authorities to inaugurate the inner kingdom he came to establish. Rather, they are responsible to accept him as their king, to prepare their hearts for him. They need faith, not control over events. The Pharisees are not prepared to do that, so they miss the kingdom. They had been looking for entirely the wrong thing.

A B C D E F G H Z H' G' F' E' D' C' B' A'

Messiah not securable (17:22)

"And he said to the disciples, 'The days are coming when you will desire to see one of the days of the Son of man, and you will not see it.'"

Notice that Jesus now turns to the disciples. The Pharisees doubtless hear his words, but they are not spoken to them. Although Jesus insists that his kingdom is already present, he turns the topic to future events. There will come a day when his followers want him to be with them physically, but he will not be available. This is not the only time in Scripture that Jesus speaks of his future absence. He will leave, and they will not be able to follow. He will go, but he will

---

271 St. Bede, quoted in Aquinas, *Catena Aurea*, Luke 17:21. Also, Romans 10:8.
272 Theophylact of Ohrid, quoted in Lapide, *The Great Commentary*, Luke 21:21.

send the Comforter to them. They should rejoice while he is with them, because the day will come when they will fast because of his absence.[273]

So, even though the kingdom is present, soon the king will be un-findable. His followers will pine for him, but he will not be physically accessible in the same manner he is now. This is certainly a puzzling turn in the conversation. Perhaps this conversation helps us to understand why the disciples were so confused a few days later in Matthew 23-25. They needed the more straightforward two-answer format of the Olivet Discourse to make sense of it all. Even then it could be confusing.

The language here in Luke—"*you will not see it*"—implies what Jesus will state clearly in Matthew: The wait for the Second Advent will be a long one. You will experience death before you witness my return. The cry of *maranatha!* continues to well up in the souls of all loyal Christians; at the same time, we must all be aware that we may not see him this side of death.

The impending long absence does not mean that Christ will neglect his people. There is more to this discourse. As St. Bede wrote, "Well does Christ say that he shall be revealed as one who, not being seen, sees all things, and then appearing, shall judge all things."[274]

A B C D E F G H Z H' G' F' E' D' C' B' A'

Pursuit (17:23)

"And they will say to you, 'Lo, there!' or 'Lo, here!' Do not go, do not follow them."

---

273 John 14:1-29, Matthew 9:15.
274 St. Bede, quoted in Lapide, *The Great Commentary*, Luke 17:30.

Jesus knew the human soul. He knew that during the long wait between his Ascension and his Second Coming many people would not be satisfied to wait in faith. Messianic movements would arise that would claim, "Look, here is the messiah!" or "The kingdom is being formed over there, around that christ!" But neither the First nor the Second Advent would work out according to human expectations, as we know from Matthew. If someone told the disciples that Christ had returned after the Ascension, they were not to listen. Christ would not return in that manner.

But this was a difficult message to swallow. The Jews wanted a political kingdom that would defend them from the Romans (and Egyptians, and Persians). We can certainly understand: Some Christians today pine for Christ to reign in temporal glory. Segment E makes it clear that false messiahs will prey on those longings. Here, and a few days later in Matthew, Jesus warns that these impostors offering false hope do not represent him. Christians must not follow after these men.

False messiahs are a bigger issue in Matthew than here. Remember that the Pharisees are still listening, and in some ways they were similar to modern-day political operatives. Whatever Jesus says, they will try to spin it to their own purposes. Soon they will put Jesus on trial and attempt to use his own words against him. Jesus knows that they will not take to heart any warnings about false messiahs, because they don't even believe the true messiah is in their midst. Jesus has already established the parameters for public discourse—"Do not give dogs what is holy; and do not throw your pearls before swine, lest they trample them under foot and turn to attack you" (Matt. 7:6)—and in a few days he will have time to discuss the false teachers privately in more detail.

A B C D E F G H Z H' G' F' E' D' C' B' A'

Day of the Son of Man (17:24)

"For as the lightning flashes and lights up the sky from one side
to the other, so will the Son of man be in his day."

As in Matthew, Jesus contrasts the style of his Second Coming with that of the false messiahs. They will build support
in a lengthy whispering campaign. Christ will be univer-
sally and suddenly recognized by all at his Second Coming.
The final eschaton will be unmistakable. No one will need
to gin up support for Christ when he returns.

This is a good time to note another essential difference
between Matthew and Luke. In Luke we are only five verses
into an eighteen-verse dialogue, yet Jesus has already alluded to multiple comings. He started with the Incarnation
in segment B. The kingdom has come because it is present
wherever the king is, though the Pharisees missed it.

In segment C, Jesus said, "the kingdom of God is in the
midst of you." This is still true, for this statement encompasses
the middle comings we already noted; including Christ's coming in the sacraments, in the Word, in his Spirit, and in his
holy people. Indeed, being in the "midst" aptly describes the
unfolding of his kingdom in history up to the final eschaton.

Now, in segment F, Jesus refers to the lightning. This
word picture describes the Second Advent.[275] Jesus is including all types of comings in this discourse; in fact, he moves
fluidly between them. The material is not segregated into
two answers as neatly as it is in Matthew.

---

275 Eusebius, "For as the lightning . . . He will not appear walking upon the earth, as any
common man, but will illuminate our whole universe, manifesting to all men the radiance of His divinity." Quoted in Aquinas, *Catena Aurea*, Luke 17:22-25.

The only coming not mentioned yet in this dialogue is the coming in judgment. But Jesus will get there in a few more segments.

A B C D E F G H Z H' G' F' E' D' C' B' A'

Suffering (17:25)

"But first he must suffer many things and be rejected by this generation."

Christ will come again in glory. But suffering must come first. Although the glorious Second Coming is still a ways off at an indeterminable time, the suffering of the Passion is close by. Jesus does not predict his glorious coming within a generation, but he *does* predict that his suffering will occur within that time. The very men surrounding him at that moment will reject their Messiah.

There are two reasons this statement is important and relevant. First, his disciples are still under the impression (as we saw when we examined Luke 19) that Jesus will be crowned king of David's reconstituted kingdom when they enter Jerusalem. After all, Jesus has just said that "the kingdom of God is in the midst of you." They could misunderstand this statement, and the triumphal entry in a few days will only feed that delusion.[276] So, Jesus speaks about what will really happen. He will be rejected and "suffer many things." "He said this . . . lest the Apostles, seeing Him suffering and being put to death on the cross, should be offended, and doubt whether He were the Christ."[277]

---

276 St. Cyril, "His disciples supposed that He would go to Jerusalem, and would at once make a manifestation of the kingdom of God. To rid them therefore of this belief, He informs them that it became Him first to suffer the Life-giving Passion, then to ascend to the Father." Quoted in Aquinas, *Catena Aurea*, Luke 17:22-25.

277 Euthymius, quoted in Lapide, *The Great Commentary*, Luke 21:25. Also, St. Bede.

Secondly, Jesus is explaining a principle of reality. It applies to us and to his disciples. He is saying to them and to us,

"Wonder not if troubles come upon you, so great as to make you wish for the days when I was with you. For even I myself, who will come as the lightning, must first suffer many things, and be rejected, and so come into that glory. Let this be your example, for to you also shall come glory from perils."[278]

Suffering precedes glory. It is true even for the Son of God. We sometimes chafe at this reality. We resist picking up our cross and following because we don't like suffering. But Jesus found joy by embracing the cross in self-sacrificing love. It must become true for us as well.

A B C D E F G **H** Z H' G' F' E' D' C' B' A'

Eating and drinking: Noah (17:26-27a)

"As it was in the days of Noah, so will it be
in the days of the Son of man. They ate, they drank,
they married, they were given in marriage."

As Jesus knows, not all men will accept that suffering precedes glory. They are more interested in enjoyment. Noah's time illustrates this well (Gen. 6-9). Before the destruction of the flood, life was enjoyable, albeit far from holy. People were enjoying ordinary and normal things: eating, drinking, and marrying. They wouldn't have been carrying on in this comfortable way if they had believed that universal judgment was imminent.

---

278 Theophylact of Ohrid, quoted in Lapide, *The Great Commentary*, Luke 21:25.

Chrysostom, in fact, wrote that the people's infidelity, and thus their destruction, followed from their "self-indulgence."[279] What a choice lies before mankind! Suffering is to be followed by glory—or enjoyment is to be followed by destruction. It is not an appealing set of options, but it is the choice Jesus delineates.

The story of Noah describes a universal judgment.[280] The Pharisees knew it well: A worldwide rejection of God's ways precipitated a worldwide calamity, not a localized event. So, Jesus uses it as an example of the Second Advent, which will also be worldwide. In the second answer in Matthew, he used Noah in just the same way to speak of the final eschaton. Before the Second Advent, life will be comfortable and normal and enjoyable for many—so comfortable and so normal that people will lapse into unbelief. But those who reject the Son of Man will find that judgment will come.

A B C D E F G H Z H' G' F' E' D' C' B' A'

Salvation and destruction (17:27b)

*"[U]ntil the day when Noah entered the ark,
and the flood came and destroyed them all."*

This brings us to the climax of Luke's narrative. Noah was a righteous man, the only one left, living in a sinful culture. His message was rejected even though he offered the only hope of salvation. Everything seemed to be normal and ordinary until the day the flood came. Then, there was no escape for those who had not entered the ark.

When Jesus spoke to the disciples privately in Matthew, the climax involved the evangelization of the Roman Empire. But

---

279 St. John Chrysostom, quoted in Aquinas, *Catena Aurea*, Luke 17:26–30.

280 Interestingly, the story of Noah, from Genesis 6:10 to 9:19, forms a chiasm, or palistrophe.

here in Luke, Jesus is speaking in the presence of antagonistic Pharisees. Rather than focusing on the salvation provided for Noah's family, Jesus concentrates on the judgment of the sinners. He thus presents a warning to the listening Pharisees—in fact to all of us. He has already alluded to the long wait before he returns. All those that reject him will meet universal judgment, just as Noah's generation did. They may have approached Jesus to trap or embarrass him, but he turns the tables on them by presenting *them* with a choice: salvation or destruction.

At the time Jesus speaks these words, all of human experience is "upside down." It has been awry since before anyone can remember: since Adam's rejection of God. But within a few short days, reality will be put right side up again. The universal condition of sin and death caused by Adam's disobedience will be overcome. How will the world be made right again? Through the suffering of segment G.

Christ's mention of his Passion has led to a topic connected with it: our final judgment. For without his suffering, none of us could withstand that judgment. Jesus' death and resurrection are the only basis upon which any of us can hope to stand before God and be saved.

The final judgment appears as the climax of the chiasm. Here is the heart of Jesus' answer to the Pharisees who were grilling him: *You will be judged. But you need not be destroyed. Noah was saved from judgment in the ark.*[281]

A B C D E F G H Z H' G' F' E' D' C' B' A'
Eating and drinking: Lot (17:28)
"Likewise as it was in the days of Lot—they ate, they drank, they bought, they sold, they planted, they built."

---

281 The ark in the New Covenant became a symbol for the Church.

Jesus now introduces a new story. Although the transition to a new topic might be subtle and thus easy to miss, it is unmistakably there. The focus shifts from the ultimate judgment of all men at the final eschaton (Noah), to the judgment of A.D. 70. To make the transition, Jesus uses another Old Testament story: that of Abraham's nephew, Lot. Described in 2 Peter 2:7 as a righteous man, he was saved from the judgment of Sodom when he fled the city at God's command (Genesis 19).

This choice of story is the unmistakable clue that Jesus has moved from a discussion of the final eschaton to a discussion of the localized judgment of A.D. 70. Noah illustrates the final judgment because in his story the entire world is judged. But in Lot's story, only one urban culture—that of Sodom and Gomorrah—is judged and meets its doom. In Noah's day, only those in the ark provided by God's instructions are saved. In Lot's day, anyone who promptly departed the city for the safety of the mountains would be spared.

While the universality of Noah's judgment is extraordinary, the culture of Noah's time was not. Lot and his family also lived in a culture of complacency. The wicked residents of Sodom were pursuing normal pleasures. Like Noah's contemporaries (segment H) they were eating and drinking. The Sodomites were planning for the future by planting and building (segment H'). In neither case did the people give a moment's thought to any judgment that might come as a result of their misconduct.

Why is it that we expect a heads-up when trouble or judgment is on its way? What is it about human nature that caused the Pharisees to presume they had the right to know the "when" of God's timetable? Why does it seem unfair when tragedy strikes us unawares? Jesus describes reality truthfully. We leave the house every morning with nary a clue as to how the day might end. We lull ourselves into complacency by the everyday routine of the ordinary lives we live—and then something happens. Christ's return will be no different.

A B C D E F G H Z H' **G'** F' E' D' C' B' A'

Destruction (17:29)

"[B]ut on the day when Lot went out from Sodom fire and sulphur rained from heaven and destroyed them all."

The very day the angels escorted Lot's family out of sinful Sodom, fire rained down from heaven and destroyed those left in the city. Noah's generation received more warning—years of preaching by Noah—than did Lot's generation. Jesus is using Lot to warn that the impending localized judgment of A.D. 70 will entail little notice to unbelieving Jerusalemites as well.

Wait a minute—are there not eight signs to warn the Church about the destruction of Jerusalem's temple? Yes, we find them in Matthew 23-24. But that entire discourse will be given in private, meant for Christ's Church. It will not be published in the *Jerusalem Post*. It is highly unlikely that the unbelieving Pharisees ever heard Christ's words of warning as we have them in Matthew.

In segment G, "this generation" rejects Jesus. Here in segment G', the same generation will be judged as was Lot's generation. Yes, all future generations will ultimately give answer for what they decide to do about Jesus (as in Noah's story). But the generation that rejected him will experience a localized judgment in A.D. 70 (as in Lot's time).

In fact, it's quite possible that some of the Pharisees questioning him at this very moment will be among those condemning him at the Sanhedrin trial. The leadership of Jerusalem will reject its moment of grace. The generation of Jesus will miss its opportunity to accept God's gift. As a result, it will be judged as surely as Jesus will suffer. Here in Luke, Jesus does not emphasize "this generation" in the same dramatic fashion as in Matthew, but the warning is still here.

But, there is also a note of hope. Lot was hopelessly outnumbered in his generation. He could not even count on his own wife to run by his side to safety! St. Cyril of Jerusalem taught in catechism that God "despised not Lot, who was but one; how then shall He despise many righteous?"[282] Count on it: God will save every one of those who trust in him.

A B C D E F G H Z H' G' F' E' D' C' B' A'

Day of the Son of Man (17:30)

"[S]o will it be on the day when the Son of man is revealed."

This segment speaks of the coming of Christ in judgment on Jerusalem, precipitated by its rejection of the Son. But the present segment F' parallels the metaphor of the ascending segment F. In the latter, Christ's Second Advent is compared to the electric "fire" of lightning. Here, Christ's middle coming in judgment in A.D. 70 is compared to Sodom's "fire and sulfur." In both Christ is to be revealed, though in slightly different ways.

Jesus' middle coming in A.D. 70 and the final eschaton are two different events, but they are intimately linked. We can glean something about the destruction of the world by looking at the destruction of the Jerusalem temple. We will delve into this later, but the localized judgment of A.D. 70

282 Cyril, *Catechetical Lectures of St. Cyril*, 15:23.

stands as a type, a precursor to the universal judgment of the final eschaton.

At this point, all the comings have been mentioned. In this short discourse, Jesus actually speaks to all of the comings that we drew from Pope Benedict's work. By the time we read through segment F, the Incarnation, the Second Advent, and all of the middle comings except the "coming in judgment" were mentioned. Segments H' through F' discuss the "missing" middle coming in judgment. All the bases have now been covered.

A B C D E F G H Z H' G' F' **E'** D' C' B' A'

Flight (17:31)

"On that day, let him who is on the housetop,
with his goods in the house, not come down to take them away;
and likewise let him who is in the field not turn back."

Jesus uses the same illustrations here in Luke that he will repeat a few days later in Matthew. He gives the same exhortation: Do not go home to retrieve your possessions. As in Lot's day, the window of escape from Jerusalem's destruction will be very small.

Segment E' is solid confirmation that Jesus has used Lot's story to prepare his followers for the urgency of A.D. 70, and not the final eschaton. The exhortation is to flee. But flight to the mountains will not save you at the end of the world! It saved Lot because Sodom's judgment was localized. If he and his family made it to the hills, they would be saved. Flight will save the Christians in Jerusalem because that judgment is also localized.

Corresponding segment E forbade pursuing Christ when he was not physically available: "Do not run into the wilderness pursuing a false dream." Segment E' mirrors that idea; instead of forbidding pursuit, it urges flight. "*Do run into the wilderness pursuing safety. Leave all your things behind to escape the nightmare in Jerusalem!*" This is Jesus' message for the leadership of his fledgling Church.

A B C D E F G H Z H' G' F' E' D' C' B' A'
Life is not securable (17:32–33)
"Remember Lot's wife. Whoever seeks to gain his life will lose it, but whoever loses his life will preserve it."

Not all of Lot's family made it to the mountains. Lot's wife stands as an example of what not to do. She attempted to hold on to her old life in the face of God's judgment. She hesitated to obey the messengers of God, longing for the material comforts she had left behind in Sodom. The story was so well known that Jesus does not even need to fill in the details.

In like manner, when the judgment of Jerusalem arrives, it will be essential that the Christians quickly and whole-heartedly follow their bishop out of the city to safety. The window for escape will be as small as it was for Lot and his wife. Those who hesitate to obey will be lost just as surely as Lot's wife was lost. At issue here is obedience to Church authority.[283] Lot's wife was turned into a pillar of salt; the Jews who remain in Jerusalem in A.D. 70, ignoring the commands Christ gave his Church, will be turned into slaves or corpses.

---

283 St. Ambrose: "She looked back on the burning Sodom, *against the command of the angel*, and was changed into a pillar of salt, so you also, *against these commandments of mine*, may return to the life of the world, and perish with that which is perishing." Quoted in Lapide, *The Great Commentary*, Luke 21:32.

As is so often the case with Scripture, there is a larger message contained in Jesus' words here.[284] Anyone—any-time—anywhere—who clings to his worldly life will lose his eternal life. In this sense, this segment mirrors the message of segment D. There, the disciples are warned against holding onto the "physical Christ" on whom they had grown to depend. But that effort is futile; he cannot be secured. He will be physically absent, and they need to accept the spiritual nature of the kingdom.

In like manner, we must not seek to hold on to the comforts of our physical possessions. This is a difficult lesson in our materialistic culture. Possessions are never really secure, but they can keep us from a secure eternity. Christ taught, "Whoever of you does not renounce all that he has cannot be my disciple" (Luke 14:33). Indeed, there are men and women in the Church who are called to a complete renunciation of *all* worldly possessions. Although the Church does not teach that this vow of total poverty is necessary for salvation, it *is* necessary that we follow its spirit. We must strive to detach ourselves from what possessions we do have. For those who try to make their life secure will lose it.

A B C D E F G H Z H' G' F' E' D' C' B' A'

Kingdom (hidden) in your midst (17:34–35)

*"I tell you, in that night there will be two in one bed;
one will be taken and the other left. There will be two women
grinding together; one will be taken and the other left."*

---

284 St. Ambrose and St. Augustine. "What is the meaning of Lot's wife? She represents those who look back in tribulation and separate themselves from the hope of the Divine Promise." Augustine, quoted in Lapide, *The Great Commentary*, Luke 17:32.

The last segment ended with the universal principle about losing or gaining your life. This next segment picks up at that point—dealing again with the universal Day of Judgment at the Second Coming. In a sense, the entire story of Lot and his wife is a large parenthesis, necessitated by the audience of Pharisees. It begins with "likewise" in segment H', continues through segments G', F', E', and D', and ends with "remember Lot's wife." At this point the passage pivots from the temporal punishment of A.D. 70 back to the more eternal issues that made up the climax of this discourse. In segment C', the topic returns to a description of the Second Advent.

How do we know that we have left the discussion of the particular judgment on a city and reengaged the worldwide judgment? Because of the two illustrations Jesus now uses. In both, two people will be together, but only one of them will enter the eternal kingdom. The first illustration has the people in bed at night. The other illustration has people preparing their midday meal. Jesus' exhortation in E' to flee and not turn back makes sense only in the context of the localized, temporal judgment of Jerusalem in A.D. 70; but only a worldwide event spanning different time zones could encompass both nighttime and daytime activities at the same moment. (We encountered similar phrases in Matthew, where Jesus also used them to describe the situation at the final eschaton.)

In segment C, Jesus shocked the Pharisees by stating that the "kingdom of God is in the midst of you." These two illustrations in segment C' show what the kingdom being in "the midst of you" looks like: The kingdom exists in a largely *hidden* way. How strange an idea this is to the disciples: Loyal kingdom folk will be working and living next to non-kingdom folk. This is possible only if Jesus is speaking of a spiritual kingdom rather than a political one.

"But the habit of living together does not equalize the merits of men."[285] Some will be taken, while their friends and coworkers will be left. The righteous life of the godly certainly attracts those who refuse to make a commitment to God. The kingdom of God within us imbues Christians with "righteousness and peace and joy in the Holy Spirit" (Rom. 14:17). Inner peace and joy are intensely attractive. But the hangers-on will not be saved by association.

The Pharisees missed out at the First Advent because they were more concerned about control rather than submission and faith. Some Jews trapped in Jerusalem doubtless knew those Christians who were led out to safety, but did not believe enough to obediently join them. That is always the issue—faith that expresses itself in obedient action. That is why the worldly will fail to be ready for the end of the world.

A B C D E F G H Z H' G' F' E' D' C' B' A'
Kingdom's advent indiscernible (17:37a)
"And they said to him, 'Where, Lord?'"

The descending segment B' reflects the ascending segment B very well. Jesus' answer there started with the assertion that the Pharisees could not observe the coming of the kingdom with the type of signs that they demanded. They could not observe it nor control it, so they missed it. It was already there, and yet they were asking when it would appear.

In B', the disciples ask the only question left: "If the kingdom is already here, hidden in our midst, *where can we find it?*" A few days after this exchange, in Matthew, they seek insider knowledge on the destruction of the temple; they

---

285 St. Ambrose, quoted in Aquinas, *Catena Aurea*, Luke 17:34-37.

want useful information about where the kingdom can be found. Their incentive remains the same on both occasions: to gain knowledge in order to influence future events.

A B C D E F G H Z H' G' F' E' D' C' B' **A'**

Control denied (17:37b)

"He said to them, 'Where the body is, there the eagles will be gathered together.'"

Jesus' answer to the disciples is the same as it is to the Pharisees. The Pharisees in ascending segment A, and the disciples in descending segment B', are both seeking knowledge about future events. Their motive is much the same: to gain control of their situation. Humans want to think they are in control of any situation, but neither the "when" nor the "where" of ordinary life and death is under human control. This is true of the events of A.D. 70, to say nothing of the final eschaton. The Pharisees think the emerging kingdom will surely have to pass their muster. The disciples, though they have faith, do not yet understand the true meaning of Christ's kingdom and what their role in it will be. Both Pharisee and disciple seek controlling knowledge—and are denied it. But, Jesus does give them all the saving signs and knowledge they truly need.

In Matthew, we examined the backdrop of Job and the eagles, which made the theme of control very clear. But, the eagle has another significance in the Old Testament: It was a bird associated with God's judgment. In Deuteronomy 28:49, Moses warned the Israelites of the curses that would befall them if they broke the Law: "The Lord will bring a nation against you from afar, from the end of the earth, as swift as the eagle flies." Any Jewish audience would not take the mention of eagles as a good omen.

Eagles are mentioned also in Habakkuk 1:8. There, the eagles are compared to the horses of the Babylonians: "swift to devour." God tells Habakkuk that this evil nation will punish Jerusalem for him, thereby fulfilling the prophecy of eagles in Deuteronomy. Habakkuk's reaction to this news reflects Job's; he bristles at the injustice of it. But, in the face of this Babylonian threat, Habakkuk finally concludes that total trust in God's plan and will is his only option. He does not claim to understand God's judgment or seek to control Jerusalem's destiny, but chooses to trust God completely. His experience builds on Job's understanding. Job accepted God's control over the basic injustice of the seemingly random difficulties that buffeted him. Habakkuk accepted God's control over the promised judgment, explicitly emphasizing faith as the only alternative to the futility of attempting to control our own destinies.

This theme of complete faith in God is expressed in his most famous phrase: "The righteous shall live by his faith" (Hab. 2:4). That is the conclusion of Habakkuk: faith in God in the face of God's judgment. It still applies. Man is important—the most important of God's creations. But we sometimes let it go to our heads. As we learned in Matthew, the reference to the eagles of the Old Testament book of Job, which Jesus repeats here in Luke, reminds us that God is in control. Habakkuk sharpens the point of that lesson to include God's judgment. Judgment and justice are ultimately divine prerogatives. So, the final segment of the chiasm returns to the theme of mankind's impotence and God's sovereignty over life, death, judgment, and time. In the face of this reality, Habakkuk urges us to trust in almighty God. Faith in him will never disappoint.

CONCLUSION

The End Is Upon Us

We have completed our examination of the five major passages, along with some shorter incidental passages, in which Jesus discussed the end of the world. It is appropriate now to reflect on what we now know Jesus taught—and didn't teach—about the end of the world.

Christ's words are for the faithful

Since we just completed Luke 17, let's begin with that passage. You may be thinking: "This answer of Jesus in Luke 17 to the Pharisees is much too difficult to decipher by itself. Jesus alludes to all the comings: First Advent, five middle comings, and Second Advent. But they seem randomly addressed. Jesus does not even discuss them in the order of their historical emergence. There is no way the Pharisees could have adequately understood Jesus' teaching. To understand him, we needed to carefully examine the chiastic structure, and that was not enough without a thorough knowledge of the Old Testament. But even that did not suffice, because we needed insight from Matthew just to make sense of Luke. And that discourse came *after* Luke by several days."

My answer: Yes, you are correct. There is very little chance that the Pharisees could have fully understood all of what Jesus taught in Luke 17. But that was by design. Jesus never intended to give the Pharisees—or anyone else—the knowledge needed for salvation *in isolation from his Church leadership*. If a Pharisee had joined the Church (as some did—see Acts 15:5), then he would have been saved in A.D. 70, because the apostles had the knowledge gleaned from Matthew 23-25 and elsewhere.

Ordinarily, there is no salvation without a commitment to the entire message of Jesus—and that includes a commitment to the Church he established. The necessity of Church guidance does not apply only to salvation from Jerusalem's destruction in A.D. 70. We need the Church to enliven us, nourish us, guide us, and lead us home. It is to us what the ark was to Noah.

We need the Church's help in the study of the sacred text as well. When we approach Scripture to unlock its meaning, we must carefully consider the context and seek the Church's guidance. In failing to do this, Russell, Schweitzer, Lewis, and others end up accusing a perfect teacher of being in error. But he was not—they were. (I do not seek to be harsh in this. I write as one who did not reconcile to the Church until the age of forty.[286]) We are all at different points on a pilgrimage, and we all need to make more progress. But the person attempting to follow Christ apart from the wisdom of the Church is in the same plight as the Pharisees: He wants control over his own affairs. That did not work out well for the Pharisees in Luke 17, and it will not work out well for anyone at any time.

Different climaxes

We spent most of our time examining three long passages that are organized in chiasms: the first answer to the disciples contained in Matthew 23-24, the second answer to the disciples in Matthew 24-25, and the answer to the Pharisee in Luke

---

286 For details of my pilgrimage into the Church, see David B. Currie, *Born Fundamentalist, Born Again Catholic* (San Francisco, CA: Ignatius Press, 1996).

17. Though they are organized in similar literary structures, as we noted, they have two very different audiences. In Luke, a Pharisee asks mockingly when he will notice any evidence of a new kingdom of God. In contrast, both of the answers in Matthew are in response to the four closest disciples privately asking Jesus for help in understanding.

The different audiences necessitate different emphases. The climax of Luke 17 is this: Make no mistake; there will be a final judgment, and you are in danger. People of faith will be saved in the ark that God provides in the Church. The Pharisees could have understood that much at least. We may feel in control, on top of the world, but eventually judgment day will overtake each one of us. We will give an account of what we have done in response to Jesus Christ. That is a good summary of the climax of Matthew's second answer as well, though the emphasis in Luke is aimed at those who reject Christ.

The climax to the first answer of Matthew 23-24 is dramatically different. Since Jesus is in a private dialogue with loyal disciples, this makes sense. The answer is focused on the destruction of the temple in Jerusalem, and the climax is this: You must penetrate civilization with the gospel before a generation passes. Only then will the old temple cult be dismantled. The Pharisee is given a warning, but the disciples are charged with a *task*. This task of evangelization is the seventh of the eight signs, and the only sign over which the disciples were to have any control.

The two groups—believers and unbelievers—are given the information in the climax that most pertains to their situation. But, they are really two sides of the same coin. The believer must preach the gospel, and all will be judged in the end on how they respond to that gospel. Both preacher and audience will face the Judge.

The timing of the end

As for our initial question, the evidence is clear that Jesus did not predict the end of the world within a generation. When discussing the final eschaton, he repeatedly spoke of delays, a long interval of his absence, and even intervening death. His followers initially believed that the public advent of the kingdom (and thus the end of the age) was imminent—that it would occur well before a generation passed. But he spoke repeatedly of the long interregnum when his loyal people would need to work, multiply their talents, and remain watchful. There is no evidence Jesus believed the end of the world would occur soon. With the coming of the Holy Spirit, it is evident that the apostles understood this as well.

Jesus did, however, unambiguously predict, before the end of a generation, the end of the *world of the Jewish temple*. On this prophecy he staked his reputation. "Heaven and earth will pass away, but my words will not pass away" (Matt. 24:35).

The bedrock trustworthiness of his prediction should worry skeptics like Russell but bring comfort to uneasy Christians such as Schweitzer and Lewis. They can relax—no need for embarrassment or rationalization. It was not a gaffe when Jesus spoke of the future. He spoke the truth of reality. We can trust everything he taught. We *must* trust him completely.

This brings us to our Catholic college student. She, like the three others, believed Jesus was mistaken. She was taught that Christ's Church followed him in that error and only later woke up and realized it. Given that assumption, she was waiting for the Church to "wake up" again and adjust its moral teaching to accommodate abortion, contraception, divorce, and the like.

But her original premise was wrong: Jesus and his Church were not wrong about the end of the world. They were right

then, and they are right now. Jesus taught the first generation of Church leadership the truth. Subsequent generations
of leaders guarded, developed, and handed on that revealed
truth. This includes his words about his Second Advent and
the final judgment, and it includes the moral teachings that
the world so reviles today.

The end is . . . here

Every generation is in its own A.D. 70 Jerusalem. We all face
the destruction of our entire lives when we die. The only
way to escape our own personal destruction is through the
guidance of the Church. Church leadership guided the early
Christians out of a doomed Jerusalem by heeding the teaching of Jesus. It can do the same for us in every generation.

This brings us to the present situation: our own generation in the twenty-first century. What do we know about
the future? Do we know anything other than that it will be
a long wait? After all, it has *already* been a long wait for the
return of Christ!

Perhaps the best way to start is to discuss a term that is
bandied about these days but widely misunderstood: the "end
times." What exactly do the end times and the related phrase,
the "last days," mean? On this, the Church has been clear
from the beginning: The Incarnation, Passion, Resurrection,
and Ascension ushered humanity into the end times. If you
need to put secular dates to that, it falls somewhere in the
range of 4 B.C. to A.D. 70. The end times began immediately
after the transitional time of the Incarnation.

As the *Catechism* puts it:

On the threshold of his Passion Jesus announced the coming destruction of this splendid building [the temple], of
which there would not remain 'one stone upon another.'

By doing so, he announced a sign of the last days, which were *to begin with his own Passover.*[287]

Yes, that means humanity has been in the "end times" for almost 2,000 years! Which means the Church does not use the phrase in the same manner as does the bearded man on the street corner with a placard reading, "The end is near!" The bearded man seems to believe that he lives in the end times, but that his parents and grandparents did not.

With the events put in play by the Incarnation—by the coming of the Messiah promised in the Old Testament—"God's plan has entered into its fulfillment. We are already at 'the last hour.'"[288] So, Pope John Paul II could say,

> For Christians the *'eschaton,'* that is, the final event, is to be understood not only as a future goal, but as a reality which *has already begun* with the historical coming of Christ. His Passion, death, and Resurrection are the supreme event in the history of mankind, which has now entered its final phase.[289]

Thus, St. Paul could say that the Old Testament stories "were written down for our instruction, upon whom the end of the ages has come" (1 Cor. 10:11). And in Hebrews we read that "in these last days he [God the Father] has spoken to us by a Son" (Heb. 1:2).

This means that "already the final age of the world is with us, and the renewal of the world is irrevocably under way."[290]

---

287 *Catechism*, 585.
288 *Catechism*, 670.
289 Pope John Paul II, "Second Coming at the End of Time" (General Audience, April 22, 1998), 1.
290 *Catechism*, 670.

But, this renewal is being resisted by evil. Remember that Jesus predicted that he would be seated at the Father's right hand while his enemies are made his footstool. That is the stage in which we now live. "This reign is still under attack by the evil powers, even though they have been defeated definitively by Christ's Passover." The Church "herself takes her place among the creatures which groan and travail yet and await the revelation of the sons of God."[291]

So we, like the faithful servants and wise maidens in the parables, are to work for the Master, keep our lamps filled with the oil of good works, and pray for his return. Presently, "Christians pray, above all in the Eucharist, to hasten Christ's return by saying to him: Maranatha! 'Our Lord, come!'"[292]

The Second Coming could occur at any moment, and we pray for precisely that. Yet, the Church is aware that the final eschaton could be delayed another fifty generations or more.

Since the Ascension Christ's coming in glory has been imminent. . . . This eschatological coming could be accomplished at any moment, even if both it and the final trial that will precede it are "delayed."[293]

The Church is ever mindful of the admonition of Christ, "It is not for you to know times or seasons which the Father has fixed by his own authority" (Acts 1:7). No human—regardless of how savvy, smart, or saintly—can be privy to that knowledge. "The glorious Messiah's coming is suspended at every moment of history."[294] As far as the "when," that is the best we can do—or should want to do.

291 *Catechism*, 671.
292 *Catechism*, 671.
293 *Catechism*, 673.
294 *Catechism*, 674.

Our own Passion

Note how the *Catechism* links the "eschatological coming" of the Second Advent to "the final trial that will precede it." That might give you pause: Who said anything about a final trial? And if that must come first, why do we continually pray *maranatha*?

To answer this question, we must return to a principle of reality that we have discussed briefly: Suffering precedes glory; scattering precedes renewal; death precedes new life; Passion precedes Resurrection. By taking on human nature and becoming man, Christ was subject to this principle, and so must everyone be who wishes to imitate him. We experience this death and resurrection first at baptism—when we die to sin and come through the water as a new creature with supernatural life.[295] We will undergo it again at physical death, when each of us dies and enters eternal life as our hope promises us.

This principle also applies to the mystical body of Christ, the Church, which also must experience this cycle of death and resurrection. The *Catechism* identifies Christ's Passion as a type of what must happen to the Church in the final eschaton and promises that as the Second Advent approaches, persecution will intensify:

> Before Christ's second coming the Church must pass through a final trial. . . . The persecution that accompanies her pilgrimage on earth will unveil the "mystery of iniquity." . . . The Church will enter the glory of the kingdom only through this final Passover, when *she will follow her Lord in his death and Resurrection*. The kingdom

---

295 "Through the power of the Holy Spirit we take part in Christ's Passion by dying to sin, and in his Resurrection by being born to a new life." *Catechism*, 1988.

will be fulfilled, then, not by a historic triumph of the Church through a progressive ascendancy, but only by God's victory over the final unleashing of evil.[296]

"*Wait one minute,*" you might be thinking. Jesus taught repeatedly that life would be normal—as in Noah's day—when the Second Coming arrived. What is all this talk of impending trial and tribulation? Let's clarify. We did not make too much of it earlier, but it is society at large that is presented as living normal, enjoyable lives as the judgment looms, not the faithful in particular. Noah certainly wasn't! His life entailed building a massive boat, preaching to those who came to gawk, and undoubtedly enduring their ridicule.

An "ordinary" life for those that follow Christ will commonly, even necessarily, entail persecution. (Talk about a "new normal"!) The world hated Christ, and we are to pick up our cross daily and follow in his footsteps. He told us,

If the world hates you, know that it has hated me before it hated you. . . . "A servant is not greater than his master." If they persecuted me, they will persecute you (John 15:18-20).

It is perfectly congruous that the faithful endure tribulation while the rest of the culture appears to be living normal, enjoyable lives.

This is the outworking of the principle of death and resurrection. The first-century Church endured the Great Tribulation while anticipating the middle coming in judgment of A.D. 70. That set the stage for its own re-gathering and renewal. Just so, the Church awaits the Second Advent, the final eschaton, while enduring its own tribulation. The

296 *Catechism,* 675-677.

final persecution will follow the pattern of Nero in the Great Tribulation: vicious, unjust, maniacal, and deadly. Nothing, however, may be known about timing.

Did the Ukrainian Christians believe they were in the final persecution under Stalin? Did the English Catholics think that they were facing the final eschaton during the reign of Queen Elizabeth? Did Poles think Hitler might have been the Antichrist? Did the Catholics of France believe that the Reign of Terror was the end? Did Chinese Christians view Mao's terrors as the final assault? Did Mexicans wonder if President Calles might not be setting the stage for the final trial of the Church? Of course all of them might have. And for those who died, it *was* their final persecution. All of these stand—with the Great Tribulation—as a foretaste of the final assault on the Church just before the Second Coming.

Even now, Christians are suffering horrific persecution at the hands of anti-Christian regimes throughout the world. (Iran, North Korea, and China come to mind immediately.) Bishops, priests, and converts are particular targets. At times, the governments are not directly involved, but they turn a blind eye to violence. The year 2011 began with a Muslim attack on a Coptic Church in Egypt that killed twenty-one Christian worshippers. The year ended with attacks on two Nigerian churches that killed another thirty-seven. There is no need to enumerate every incident or every country: Simply check the international news during any given week. These Christian brothers and sisters are undergoing their own version of the Great Tribulation.

Less violent—but more insidious—is the persecution of Christians residing in Western democracies. It seems as though a day never passes but that someone publicly attacks our values and practices. Pundits and entertainers think it a sign of sophistication to malign Christian—especially Catholic—values and beliefs. Western nations with long traditions of religious liberty are increasingly using the law to punish or coerce those who refuse to compromise Christian ideals that conflict with the sacred cows of secularism.

Are we living in the final generation? That is not our call to make. Remember, the day and the hour is not knowable. It must have seemed as black as it could get in Stalin's Ukraine, or Hitler's Poland, or Mao's China, or Omar al-Bashir's Sudan. It is not untoward to compare our tribulation to the last one, or even to wonder aloud whether ours may indeed be that final one. But that is different than saying it *is* the final generation, or setting a time for the final eschaton, which is not our place to know or try to discover. Our duty as faithful stewards is to endure to the end, which could come at any time without warning.[297]

What the future *may* hold

The end of the world will come like lightning. And yet, Christ's words don't leave us *entirely* clueless about the events leading to his Second Advent. As you may be noticing, much of what the Church knows about the end of the world is based on the fulfillment of *types*. In a nutshell, everything that has happened in salvation history can also point to the future.

Think of Old Testament stories that have a reflection or fulfillment in a New Testament event. Jonah was in the belly of the fish for three days, which stands as a type of Jesus in the belly of the tomb for three days. Another example:

---

297 Endurance does not imply grimness. So Michael Novak could joke, "The pessimist says, 'Oh, things could never get any worse,' while the optimist says, 'Oh, yes they can!'" Yet at the same time, "No Christian can be a pessimist, for Christianity is a system of radical optimism." Marcia Segelstein, "Courage & Conversion: An Interview with Hadley Arkes," *Crisis Magazine*, August 16, 2012. And W.R. Inge, *Church and the Age* (Whitefish, MT: Kessinger Publishing, 2003), xiii.

Adam is a figure of Christ, while Eve is a figure of Mary (actually they are both antitypes, or opposites). The prophets Moses and Samuel give a foretaste of what Christ will do, while Hannah is a precursor of Mary. These are but a few examples of types in the Old Testament that find fulfillment in the New. The list is long indeed.[298]

The temple was a microcosm of the earth. Its destruction gives clues to how God works. For our discussion, although Christ's prophecies had their fulfillment in the events of A.D. 70, they also point—as a type—to the final eschaton. In A.D. 70, the Jewish world ended. At the Second Advent, the entire world will end. Thus, the eight signs that preceded the destruction of the temple can—in a limited sense—legitimately be applied to the end of the world. (The obvious exception relates to timing. Jesus ruled out any chance that any human would ever know the "when" of the final eschaton.)

Falling away

The Church teaches that the final persecution will be a kind of near-death experience for Christ's mystical body on earth—so intense that many will lose their faith. Apostasy will decimate the ranks of the faithful. "Before Christ's second coming the Church must pass through a final trial *that will shake the faith of many believers.*"[299] Today, in a Western world where Christian churches are emptying at an alarming rate, we certainly see evidence of St. Paul's statement that "in later times some will depart from the faith by giving heed to deceitful spirits and doctrines of demons" (1 Tim. 4:1).

Is this apostasy the final one? We don't know. Ultimately, it doesn't matter. None of us will be here in another two or

---

298 For an explanation of type in Scripture, see *Rapture*, 60-63.
299 *Catechism*, 675-677.

three generations, so the apostasy that we face is *our* final one. Just as in A.D. 70, our task is to resist falling away; to work and be faithful as best we can.[300] Our task is to continue the spreading of the gospel throughout civilization in every way possible. That has not really changed in 2,000 years, has it?

False teachers

What would apostasy look like without a false teacher? They seem to go hand in hand, and so the *Catechism* treats them that way.

> Before Christ's second coming . . . the "mystery of iniquity" [will arrive] in the form of a religious deception offering men an apparent solution to their problems at the price of apostasy from the truth. The supreme religious deception is that of the Antichrist.[301]

We have been promised that false messiahs were not limited to the time surrounding the temple's destruction but will continue to appear. Their appeal will always be similar: a solution apart from God's way. They will say, "Follow me, I have the answer to your troubles! You just have to compromise on your faith."

---

300 Please do not read a "simple works salvation" into this. The Church has always been clear on the balance, "Without faith it is impossible to please God. . . . It follows that no one can ever achieve justification without it, neither can anyone attain eternal life unless he or she perseveres in it to the end."*Dogmatic Constitution on the Catholic Faith, Dei Filius*: First Vatican Council (Vatican, 1890), 3:9. Also, "He that shall persevere to the end, he shall be saved. . . . Knowing that they are born again unto a hope of glory, but not as yet unto glory, they ought to fear for the combat which yet remains."*Decree Concerning Justification, De Justificatione*: Council of Trent (Vatican: 1547), 6:13. Also, Augustine, *Treatise on The Gift of Perseverance*; and secondly in Augustine, *Treatise On Rebuke and Grace*, both in Schaff, *Nicene and Post-Nicene Fathers*, vol. 5.

301 *Catechism*, 675.

As in the first century, some of the worst false teachers will arise within the Church. If you have been paying attention at all in the first decade of this century, and the last decade of the previous one, you know that apostates have wormed their way into the life of the Church. Pope Benedict XVI himself said, "Today we see in a really terrifying way that the greatest persecution of the Church does not come from the enemies outside, but is born from the sin in the Church."[302]

Of course, the false messiahs get progressively worse as time wears on. This will culminate in the Antichrist:

> The supreme religious deception is that of the Antichrist, a pseudo-messianism by which man glorifies himself in place of God. . . . The Antichrist's deception already begins to take shape in the world every time the claim is made to realize within history that messianic hope which can only be realized beyond history through the eschatological judgment. . . . Especially . . . perverse [is the] political form of a secular messianism.[303]

If we look elsewhere in the New Testament, we discover that this Antichrist will attempt his own version of Daniel's "abomination of desolation." He will attempt to gain control of the worship in the Church, the New Temple.[304] Here

---

302 *"Pope Issues His Most Direct Words to Date,"* New York Times, May 11, 2012.

303 *Catechism*, 675-677, alluding to Pope Pius XI: "Communism...conceals in itself a false messianic idea. A pseudo-ideal of justice...with a deceptive mysticism, which...entrap[s] by delusive promises." Pius XI, *Divini Redemptoris: Divine Redeemer* (Vatican: Encyclical, 1937), 8. Also alluding to Vatican 2, "Modern atheism...anticipates the liberation of man especially through his economic and social emancipation...The Church...cannot cease repudiating...those poisonous doctrines." *Pastoral Constitution on the Church in the Modern World, Gaudium et Spes:* Second Vatican Council (Vatican, 1965), 1, 1:20-21.

304 The Greek word Paul used for "temple" here is *naos*. It *always* refers to the Church in his letters. For a complete discussion, see Currie, Rapture, 208-213.

is how St. Paul describes it. I inserted the bracketed words to help clarify his meaning.

> [Christ's return] will not come, unless the rebellion comes first, and the man of lawlessness is revealed, the son of perdition, who opposes and exalts himself against every . . . object of worship, so that he takes his seat in the temple of God [the Church], proclaiming himself to be God. . . . The coming of the lawless one [will be a] wicked deception for those who are to perish, because they refused to love the truth and so be saved (2 Thess. 2:3-12).

What will this look like precisely? It is difficult to say. We do know that the attack will be on the *Church's faith and worship*. It will probably be fairly apparent at the time. The Antichrist will seek to control and subvert the Church's worship and message. He will create his own "desolating sacrilege" by attempting to replace God's will and way with his own.

The New Testament writers warned that false teachers—antichrists—would continually plague the Church. History has shown them to be correct. Never has the Church been entirely free of those who distort the truth of the gospel for their own advantage. And it will only get worse until the Antichrist.

Of course, this does bring up an important point. Apostasy, falling away, and false teachers will increase as time progresses toward the final persecution before the final eschaton. How do we know if we are indeed enduring in the truth of Christ? This can be a thorny question. Although Jesus does not address it directly in the Olivet Discourse, the answer is clear elsewhere.

There are always two groups we encounter: Christ's faithful disciples who shepherd their followers, and the false prophets who mislead their followers. To be certain that we are on the right side, we need to look at the lineage of our leaders. Do they stand in the long line of those who have followed the original Twelve? When Origen spoke of enduring to the end, he was careful to note, "He who can abide firmly in the Apostolic tradition, he shall be saved."[305] The successor to Peter will lead us to safety just as the true apostles of Christ led the Christians to safety in A.D. 70.

We have persecutions, false teachers, apostasy, and sacrilegious desolations. This all sounds very much like the eight signs of A.D. 70, doesn't it? As Mark Twain is said to have noted, "History may not repeat itself, but it rhymes a lot."[306] So, the final eschaton will resemble the end of Jerusalem. The end of the world will look familiar to anyone who has studied the destruction of the temple.

We must be careful, however. We cannot assume from the details of Matthew, Mark, and Luke that the Antichrist will appear in the wilderness of Judea, or that he will be of Jewish origin, or that he will try to raise an actual army, or that Jerusalem will be central to any major events. Specific details of that sort cannot be gleaned from types. Above all, we cannot infer a day or an hour from the signs meant for A.D. 70. Jesus clearly did not intend to give us that information. The details of the signs in the Olivet Discourse relate to the primary fulfillment, which culminated in A.D. 70. Even when words rhyme, they still remain distinct words with different meanings.

Evangelization

This brings us to the final sign in which A.D. 70 is a type of the final eschaton: evangelization. The climax of answer

---

305 Origen, cited in *Catena Aurea,* on Matthew 24:9-14.

306 This well-known misquote is a shortening of "It is not worthwhile to try to keep history from repeating itself, for man's character will always make the preventing of the repetitions impossible." Mark Twain, *Mark Twain in Eruption: Hitherto Unpublished Pages About Men and Events*, ed., Bernard DeVoto (New York: Harper, 1940).

one, in Matthew 23–24, predicted the dissemination of the gospel throughout the Roman Empire before the temple's destruction. The task of evangelizing the world in which we now live is still before us, and the Church has applied itself to the task. We must all strive to evangelize—and often now to re-evangelize—our culture before the final eschaton.

Of course, Jesus spoke forcefully about evangelization elsewhere. In fact, the very last words of Jesus that Matthew records are these:

> "Go therefore and make disciples of all nations, baptizing them in the name of the Father and of the Son and of the Holy Spirit, teaching them to observe all that I have commanded you; and lo, I am with you always, to the close of the age" (Matt. 28:19–20).

In these two verses, Jesus links his command to evangelize with his presence "to the close of the age." The Great Commission stands on its own, pointing us to the same conclusion: The world must be evangelized. It is possible to see a double application in the climax (Z) of Matthew's first answer. Indeed, St. Thomas Aquinas did, and he applied it to both A.D. 70 and the final eschaton. The primary interpretation remains its application to the generation of the apostles, with a secondary application to the generations that wait for the Second Advent.[307] Others have emphasized the latter, perhaps at the expense of the former.[308] But whether

---

307 "It is possible to maintain both applications of the passage, if only we will take this diffusion of Gospel preaching in a double sense." Aquinas, gloss, *Catena Aurea*, Matthew 24:9–14.

308 Origen, St. Jerome, and St. Augustine may seem to imply that this is the *primary* meaning of this passage. But it can be difficult to exactly determine their meaning on this issue. Origen wrote concerning this verse, "When every nation shall have heard the preaching of the Gospel, then shall come the end of the world." St. Jerome wrote, concerning this verse, "The sign of the Lord's second coming is, that the Gospel shall be

or not this is the primary meaning of Jesus is moot, since we now live "post-temple-destruction."

The Great Commission at the end of Matthew stands on its own, connecting the preaching of the gospel with the "close of the age." With or without the climax of Matthew 23-24, we must preach until Christ returns. Looking at it at least as a type, we can understand the climax of Matthew 23-24 as applying to us. Evangelizing the world is our task while we wait for the final eschaton. As Paul wrote to St. Timothy, "I charge you . . . preach the word, be[ing] urgent in season and out of season" (1 Tim. 4:1-2). We cannot wiggle off that hook.

All of us will see the end

Nowhere did Jesus predict that his Second Advent would usher in the end of the world within a generation. Whenever Jesus did mention the timing of his coming in final judgment, we notice he talked of *delay*. He spoke of a long time. He spoke of keeping watch because of its unpredictability. In fact, he implied that the generation of his disciples would *not* see the "days of the Son of Man." The evidence shows unambiguously that he taught that the final eschaton would not be soon.

What he did predict within that time, however, was the total destruction of the Jerusalem temple. To help them during that generation of the Great Tribulation, Jesus gave his disciples—the leaders of his new Church—eight signs to encourage and instruct his people. They could observe them as signposts on the road to Jerusalem's impending judgment.

---

preached in all the world, so that all may be without excuse." St. Augustine wrote, "If then we know not when it shall be that the whole world shall be filled with the Gospel, undoubtedly we know not when the end shall be; but it shall not be before such time." All in Aquinas, *Catena Aurea*, Matthew 24:9-14.

Jesus was correct about the destruction of Jerusalem, and he was correct about the delayed Second Advent; the timetable he laid out is unfolding exactly as he predicted. He was not mistaken. The authors of the New Testament were not misled. We can indeed trust his authority and that of his Church.

Since Jesus and the Church are trustworthy, it means that we will face a final judgment. Christ *will* come *for you* within a generation. None of us will get out of this alive. The end is always present for every individual in every generation. It is good advice to "remember the end of your life . . . remember destruction and death . . . remember the commandments . . . remember the covenant of the Most High" (Sir. 28:6–7).[309]

We will all face our own judgment soon—a few short decades at the most. The most important question, then, is not when the world will end, but whether we will be in a faithful state when *our* world ends. "Be alert at all times, praying that you may have the strength to escape all these things that will take place, and to stand before the Son of Man" (Luke 21:36). *Maranatha!*

---

309 Note that the "remembering" of God's written revelation is linked to preparation for the end. Pope Benedict XVI has emphasized Scripture as an aid to perseverance. "We must rediscover a taste for feeding ourselves on the word of God, faithfully handed down by the Church, and on the bread of life, offered as sustenance for his disciples." Pope Benedict XVI, *Porta Fidei: Door of Faith* (Vatican: Apostolic Letter, 2011), 3. This book is the effort of this author, however insignificant, to answer that call.

APPENDIX A

Matthew 23:36–24:35

"Truly, I say to you, all this will come upon this generation. O Jerusalem, Jerusalem, killing the prophets and stoning those who are sent to you! How often would I have gathered your children together as a hen gathers her brood under her wings, and you would not! Behold, your house is forsaken and desolate. For I tell you, you will not see me again, until you say, 'Blessed is he who comes in the name of the Lord.'"

Jesus left the temple and was going away, when his disciples came to point out to him the buildings of the temple. But he answered them, "You see all these, do you not? Truly, I say to you, there will not be left here one stone upon another, that will not be thrown down." As he sat on the Mount of Olives, the disciples came to him privately, saying, "Tell us, when will this be, and what will be the sign of your coming and of the close of the age?"

And Jesus answered them, "Take heed that no one leads you astray. For many will come in my name, saying, 'I am the Christ,' and they will lead many astray. And you will hear of wars and rumors of wars; see that you are not alarmed; for this must take place, but the end is not yet. For nation will rise against nation, and kingdom against kingdom, and there will be famines and earthquakes in various places: all this is but the beginning of the birth-pangs.

"Then they will deliver you up to tribulation, and put you to death; and you will be hated by all nations for my name's sake. And then many will fall away, and betray one another, and hate one another. And many false prophets will arise and lead many astray. And because wickedness is multiplied, most men's love will grow cold. But he who endures to the end will be saved. And this gospel of the kingdom will be preached throughout the whole world, as a testimony to all nations; and then the end will come.

"So when you see the desolating sacrilege spoken of by the prophet Daniel, standing in the holy place (let the reader understand), then let those who are in Judea flee to the mountains; let him who is on the housetop not go down to take what is in his house; and let him who is in the field not turn back to take his mantle. And alas for those who are with child and for those who give suck in those days! Pray that your flight may not be in winter or on a sabbath. For then there will be great tribulation, such as has not been from the beginning of the world until now, no, and never will be. And if those days had not been shortened, no human being would be saved; but for the sake of the elect those days will be shortened.

"Then if any one says to you, 'Lo, here is the Christ!' or 'There he is!' do not believe it. For false Christs and false prophets will arise and show great signs and wonders, so as to lead astray, if possible, even the elect. Lo, I have told you beforehand. So, if they say to you, 'Lo, he is in the wilderness,' do not go out; if they say, 'Lo, he is in the inner rooms,' do not believe it. For as the lightning comes from the east and shines as far as the west, so will be the coming of the Son of man. Wherever the body is, there the eagles will be gathered together.

"Immediately after the tribulation of those days the sun will be darkened, and the moon will not give its light, and the stars will fall from heaven, and the powers of the heavens will be shaken; then will appear the sign of the Son of man in heaven, and then all the tribes of the earth will mourn, and they will see the Son of man coming on the clouds of heaven with power and great glory; and he will send out his angels with a loud trumpet call, and they will gather his elect from the four winds, from one end of heaven to the other.

"From the fig tree learn its lesson: as soon as its branch becomes tender and puts forth its leaves, you know that summer is near. So also, when you see all these things, you know that he is near, at the very gates. Truly, I say to you, this generation will not pass away till all these things take place.

"Heaven and earth will pass away, but my words will not pass away."

Matthew 24:36–25:46

"But of that day and hour no one knows, not even the angels of heaven, nor the Son, but the Father only. As were the days of Noah, so will be the coming of the Son of man. For as in those days before the flood they were eating and drinking, marrying and giving in marriage, until the day when Noah entered the ark, and they did not know until the flood came and swept them all away, so will be the coming of the Son of man. Then two men will be in the field; one is taken and one is left. Two women will be grinding at the mill; one is taken and one is left.

"Watch therefore, for you do not know on what day your Lord is coming. But know this, that if the householder had known in what part of the night the thief was coming, he would have watched and would not have let his house be broken into. Therefore you also must be ready; for the Son of man is coming at an hour you do not expect.

"Who then is the faithful and wise servant, whom his master has set over his household, to give them their food at the proper time? Blessed is that servant whom his master when he comes will find so doing. Truly, I say to you, he will set him over all his possessions. But if that wicked servant says to himself, 'My master is delayed,' and begins to beat his fellow servants, and eats and drinks with the drunken, the master of that servant will come on a day when he does not expect him and at an hour he does not know, and will punish him, and put him with the hypocrites; there men will weep and gnash their teeth.

"Then the kingdom of heaven shall be compared to ten maidens who took their lamps and went to meet the bridegroom. Five of them were foolish, and five were wise. For when the foolish took their lamps, they took no oil with them; but the wise took flasks of oil with their lamps. As the bridegroom was delayed, they all slumbered and slept. But at midnight there was a cry, 'Behold, the bridegroom! Come out to meet him.' Then all those maidens rose and trimmed their lamps. And the foolish said to the wise, 'Give us some of your oil, for our lamps are going out.' But the wise replied, 'Perhaps there will not be enough for us and for you; go rather to the dealers and buy for yourselves.' And while they went to buy, the bridegroom came, and those who were ready went in with him to the marriage feast; and the door was shut. Afterward the other maidens came also, saying, 'Lord, lord, open to us.' But he replied, 'Truly, I say to you, I do not know you.' Watch therefore, for you know neither the day nor the hour.

"For it will be as when a man going on a journey called his servants and entrusted to them his property; to one he gave five talents, to another two, to another one, to each according to his ability. Then he went away. He who had received the five talents went at once and traded with them; and he made five talents more. So also, he who had the two talents made two talents more. But he who had received the one talent went and dug in the ground and hid his master's money.

"Now after a long time the master of those servants came and settled accounts with them. And he who had received the five talents came forward, bringing five talents more, saying, 'Master, you delivered to me five talents; here I have made five talents more.' His master said to him, 'Well done, good and faithful servant; you have been faithful over a little, I will set you over much; enter into the joy of your master.' And he also who had the two talents came forward, saying, 'Master, you delivered to me two talents; here I have made two talents more.' His master said to him, 'Well done, good and faithful servant; you have been faithful over a little, I will set you over much; enter into the joy of your master.' He also who had received the one talent came forward, saying, 'Master, I knew you to be a hard man, reaping where you did not sow, and gathering where you did not winnow; so I was afraid, and I went and hid your talent in the ground. Here you have what is yours.' But his master answered him, 'You wicked and slothful servant! You knew that I reap where I have not sowed, and gather where I have not winnowed? Then you ought to have invested my money with the bankers, and at my coming I should have received what was my own with interest. So take the talent from him, and give it to him who has the ten talents. For to every one who has will more be given, and he will have abundance; but from him who has not, even what he has will be taken away. And cast the worthless servant into the outer darkness; there men will weep and gnash their teeth.'

"When the Son of man comes in his glory, and all the angels with him, then he will sit on his glorious throne. Before him will be gathered all the nations, and he will separate them one from another as a shepherd separates the sheep from the goats, and he will place the sheep at his right hand, but the goats at the left. Then the king will say to those at his right hand, 'Come, O blessed of my Father, inherit the kingdom prepared for you from the foundation of the world; for I was hungry and you gave me food, I was thirsty and you gave me drink, I was a stranger and you welcomed me, I was naked and you clothed me, I was sick and you visited me, I was in prison and you came to me.'

"Then the righteous will answer him, 'Lord, when did we see thee hungry and feed thee, or thirsty and give thee drink? And when did we see thee a stranger and welcome thee, or naked and clothe thee? And when did we see thee sick or in prison and visit thee?' And the King will answer them, 'Truly, I say to you, as you did it to one of the least of these my brethren, you did it to me.'

"Then he will say to those at his left hand, 'Depart from me, you cursed, into the eternal fire prepared for the devil and his angels; for I was hungry and you gave me no food, I was thirsty and you gave me no drink, I was a stranger and you did not welcome me, naked and you did not clothe me, sick and in prison and you did not visit me.'

"Then they also will answer, 'Lord, when did we see thee hungry or thirsty or a stranger or naked or sick or in prison, and did not minister to thee?' Then he will answer them, 'Truly, I say to you, as you did it not to one of the least of these, you did it not to me.'

"And they will go away into eternal punishment, but the righteous into eternal life."

APPENDIX B

Luke 17:20-37

Being asked by the Pharisees when the kingdom of God was coming, he answered them, "The kingdom of God is not coming with signs to be observed; nor will they say, 'Lo, here it is!' or 'There!' for behold, the kingdom of God is in the midst of you."

And he said to the disciples, "The days are coming when you will desire to see one of the days of the Son of man, and you will not see it. And they will say to you, 'Lo, there!' or 'Lo, here!' Do not go, do not follow them. For as the lightning flashes and lights up the sky from one side to the other, so will the Son of man be in his day. But first he must suffer many things and be rejected by this generation. As it was in the days of Noah, so will it be in the days of the Son of man. They ate, they drank, they married, they were given in marriage, until the day when Noah entered the ark, and the flood came and destroyed them all.

"Likewise as it was in the days of Lot—they ate, they drank, they bought, they sold, they planted, they built, but on the day that Lot left Sodom, it rained fire and sulfur from heaven and destroyed them all—so will it be on the day when the Son of man is revealed. On that day, let him who is on the housetop, with his goods in the house, not come down to take them away; and likewise let him who is in the field not turn back. Remember Lot's wife. Whoever seeks to gain his life will lose it, but whoever loses his life will preserve it. I tell you, in that night there will be two in one bed; one will be taken and the other left. There will be two women grinding together; one will be taken and the other left."

And they said to him, "Where, Lord?"

He said to them, "Where the body is, there the eagles will be gathered together."

Luke 19:11-27

As they heard these things, he proceeded to tell a parable, because he was near to Jerusalem, and because they supposed that the kingdom of God was to appear immediately.

He said therefore, "A nobleman went into a far country to receive a kingdom and then return. Calling ten of his servants, he gave them ten pounds, and said to them, 'Trade with these till I come.' But his citizens hated him and sent an embassy after him, saying, 'We do not want this man to reign over us.' When he returned, having received the kingdom, he commanded these servants, to whom he had given the money, to be called to him, that he might know what they had gained by trading. The first came before him, saying, 'Lord, your pound has made ten pounds more.' And he said to him, 'Well done, good servant! Because you have been faithful in a very little, you shall have authority over ten cities.' And the second came, saying, 'Lord, your pound has made five pounds.' And he said to him, 'And you are to be over five cities.' Then another came, saying, 'Lord, here is your pound, which I kept laid away in a napkin; for I was afraid of you, because you are a severe man; you take up what you did not lay down, and reap what you did not sow.'

"He said to him, 'I will condemn you out of your own mouth, you wicked servant! You knew that I was a severe man, taking up what I did not lay down and reaping what I did not sow? Why then did you not put my money into the

bank, and at my coming I should have collected it with interest?' And he said to those who stood by, 'Take the pound
from him, and give it to him who has the ten pounds.' (And
they said to him, 'Lord, he has ten pounds!')

"'I tell you, that to every one who has will more be giv-
en; but from him who has not, even what he has will be
taken away. But as for these enemies of mine, who did not
want me to reign over them, bring them here and slay them
before me.'"

Luke 21:5–36

And as some spoke of the temple, how it was adorned with
noble stones and offerings, he said, "As for these things which
you see, the days will come when there shall not be left here
one stone upon another that will not be thrown down."

And they asked him, "Teacher, when will this be, and what
will be the sign when this is about to take place?"

And he said, "Take heed that you are not led astray; for
many will come in my name, saying, 'I am he!' and, 'The
time is at hand!' Do not go after them. And when you hear
of wars and tumults, do not be terrified; for this must first
take place, but the end will not be at once." Then he said to
them, "Nation will rise against nation, and kingdom against
kingdom; there will be great earthquakes, and in various
places famines and pestilences; and there will be terrors and
great signs from heaven. But before all this they will lay
their hands on you and persecute you, delivering you up to
the synagogues and prisons, and you will be brought before
kings and governors for my name's sake. This will be a time
for you to bear testimony. Settle it therefore in your minds,
not to meditate beforehand how to answer; for I will give

you a mouth and wisdom, which none of your adversaries will be able to withstand or contradict. You will be delivered up even by parents and brothers and kinsmen and friends, and some of you they will put to death; you will be hated by all for my name's sake. But not a hair of your head will perish. By your endurance you will gain your lives.

"But when you see Jerusalem surrounded by armies, then know that its desolation has come near. Then let those who are in Judea flee to the mountains, and let those who are inside the city depart, and let not those who are out in the country enter it; for these are days of vengeance, to fulfill all that is written.

Alas for those who are with child and for those who give suck in those days! For great distress shall be upon the earth and wrath upon this people; they will fall by the edge of the sword, and be led captive among all nations; and Jerusalem will be trodden down by the Gentiles, until the times of the Gentiles are fulfilled.

"And there will be signs in sun and moon and stars, and upon the earth distress of nations in perplexity at the roaring of the sea and the waves, men fainting with fear and with foreboding of what is coming on the world; for the powers of the heavens will be shaken. And then they will see the Son of man coming in a cloud with power and great glory. Now when these things begin to take place, look up and raise your heads, because your redemption is drawing near."

And he told them a parable: "Look at the fig tree, and all the trees; as soon as they come out in leaf, you see for yourselves and know that the summer is already near. So also, when you see these things taking place, you know that the king-

dom of God is near. Truly, I say to you, this generation will
not pass away till all has taken place. Heaven and earth will
pass away, but my words will not pass away.

"But take heed to yourselves lest your hearts be weighed
down with dissipation and drunkenness and cares of this
life, and that day come upon you suddenly like a snare; for
it will come upon all who dwell upon the face of the whole
earth. But watch at all times, praying that you may have
strength to escape all these things that will take place, and
to stand before the Son of man."

APPENDIX C

Timeline of Historical Events

c. 4 B.C.	Birth of Jesus
Spring, A.D. 27	Baptism of Jesus
April, 30	Olivet Discourse
April 7, 30	Passion of Jesus (April 3, 33, has also been proposed)
May, 30	Ascension
43/44	Jewish persecution claims St. James the Greater; Mary flees to Ephesus
49/50	First Council of Jerusalem
60/63	Assumption of Mary
July, 64	Two-thirds of Rome burned down, Great Tribulation begun
July, 66	Daily sacrifice for Nero halted
Summer, 66	Attack of Cestius Gallus repelled
February, 67	War on Jerusalem declared by Nero
67-69	Vespasian waged Jewish-Roman War
June 9, 68	Suicide of Nero
July 1, 69	Vespasian declared emperor by troops (three rivals dead by the fall)
Summer, 70	Titus, Vespasian's son, waged Jewish-Roman War
August 10, 70	Temple torched (*Tisha B'Av* on ninth of Av)
Sept. 9, 70	Urban warfare in Jerusalem completed
Late Oct., 70	Slaves sorted, rebels captured or killed, Roman army disbanded
70-73	Dismantling of temple stone by stone

BIBLIOGRAPHY

Ambrose. *Exposition of the Christian Faith, Nicene and Post-Nicene Fathers.* Edited by Philip Schaff. Oxford: Parker, 1891.

Athanasius. *Against the Arians, Nicene and Post-Nicene Fathers.* Edited by Philip Schaff. Oxford: Parker, 1891.

Athanasius. *Apologia de Fuga: Defense of His Flight, Nicene and Post-Nicene Fathers.* Edited by Philip Schaff. Oxford: Parker, 1891.

Augustine. *The City of God.* Translated by Marcus Dods. New York: The Modern Library, 1950.

Augustine. *The Works of Saint Augustine: A Translation for the 21st Century: Letters 156-210,* Volume 3. Translated by Roland J. Teske. Hyde Park, NY: New City Press, 2004.

Augustine. *Treatise on Rebuke and Grace, Nicene and Post-Nicene Fathers.* Edited by Philip Schaff. Oxford: Parker, 1891.

Augustine. *Treatise On The Gift of Perseverance, Nicene and Post-Nicene Fathers.* Edited by Philip Schaff. Oxford: Parker, 1891.

Aquinas, Thomas. *Catena Aurea: Golden Chain Commentary on the Four Gospels.* Translated by John Henry Newman. Oxford: J. H. Parker, 1843.

Aquinas, Thomas. *Summa Theologica.* Translated by Fathers of the English Dominican Province. Chicago, IL: Benzinger Brothers, 1947.

Baker, Kenneth A., S.J. *The One and Triune God.* DVD. Notre Dame, IN: International Catholic University.

Barber, Michael. *Coming Soon: Unlocking the Book of Revelation and Applying Its Lessons Today.* Steubenville, OH: Emmaus Road Publishing, 2006.

Barker, Margaret. *Risen Lord (Scottish Journal of Theology.)* Edinburgh: T&T Clark, 1996.

Barker, Margaret. *The Time is Fulfilled: Jesus and the Jubilee, Scottish Journal of Theology.* Cambridge: Cambridge University Press, 2000.

Bergsma, John Sietze. *The Jubilee from Leviticus to Qumran: A History of Interpretation*. Boston: Brill, 2007.

Bruce, Frederick Fyvie. *The New Testament Documents, Are They Reliable?* Downers Grove, IL: Intervarsity Press, 1972.

Catechism of the Catholic Church. New York: Doubleday Religion, 2003.

Charles, R.H. *The Book of Enoch, or 1 Enoch*. Oxford: Parker, 1912.

Charles, R.H. *1 Enoch, The Apocrypha and Pseudepigrapha of the Old Testament*, Volume 1. Berkeley, CA: Apocryphile Press, 2004.

Chrysostom, John. *Against the Jews, in Discourses against Judaizing Christians*, in *The Fathers of the Church*. Translated by Paul W. Harkins. Washington: Catholic University of America Press, 1979.

Chrysostom, John. *Homily 75-78 on Matthew, Nicene and Post-Nicene Fathers*. Edited by Philip Schaff. Oxford: Parker, 1891.

Clement of Rome (Pope Clement I). *First Epistle of Clement to the Corinthians, Ante-Nicene Fathers: The Writings of the Fathers Down to A.D. 325*. Edited by Alexander Roberts, with James Donaldson and A. Cleveland Coxe. Edinburgh: T&T Clark, 1870.

Cook, John Granger. *The Interpretation of the Old Testament in Greco-Roman Paganism*. Tubingen, Germany: Paul Mohr Verlag, 2004.

Currie, David B. *Born Fundamentalist, Born Again Catholic*. San Francisco, CA: Ignatius Press, 1996.

Currie, David B. *Rapture: The End Times Error That Leaves the Bible Behind*. Manchester, NH: Sophia Institute Press, 2003.

Cyprian. *The Letters of St. Cyprian of Carthage: Ancient Christian Writers*, Volume 3. Edited by G.W. Clarke. Mahwah, NJ: Paulist Press, 1986.

Cyril of Alexandria. *A Commentary upon the Gospel of Luke.* Translated by R. Payne Smith. Oxford: University Press, 1859.

Cyril of Jerusalem. *Catechetical Lectures of St. Cyril, Nicene and Post-Nicene Fathers,* volume 7. Translated by Edwin Hamilton Gifford. Oxford: Parker, 1893.

Donfried, Karl Paul. *"The Allegory of the Ten Virgins as a Summary of Matthean Theology." Journal of Biblical Literature* 93 (1974):3.

Epstein, Isidore, ed. *The Babylonian Talmud.* London: Soncino Press, 1948.

Eusebius Pamphilius, *Demonstratio Evangelia: The Proof of the Gospel,* trans. W.J. Ferrar. (New York, Macmillan Company, 1920.

Eusebius Pamphilius of Caesarea. *Ecclesiastical History.* Translated by Kirsopp Lake. New York: Harvard University Press, 1980.

Frankl, Viktor Emil. *Man's Search for Meaning.* Boston: Beacon Press, 1959.

Gregory of Nazianzen. *The Theological Orations, Nicene and Post-Nicene Fathers.* Edited by Philip Schaff. Oxford: Parker, 1891.

Hahn, Scott. *A Father Who Keeps His Promises.* Ann Arbor, MI: Servant Books, 1998.

Hahn, Scott. *Kinship by Covenant: A Canonical Approach to the Fulfillment of God's Saving Promises.* New Haven, CT: Anchor Yale Bible Library, 2009.

Hahn, Scott. *The Lamb's Supper.* New York: Doubleday Religion, 1999.

Harkins, Paul W., trans., *The Fathers of the Church.* Washington: Catholic University of America Press, 1979.

Hippolytus, *The Refutation of all Heresies, Ante-Nicene Fathers: The Writings of the Fathers Down to A.D. 325.* Edited by Alexander Roberts, with James Donaldson and A. Cleveland Coxe. Edinburgh: T&T Clark, 1870.

Inge, William Ralph. *Church and the Age.* Whitefish, MT: Kessinger Publishing, 2003.

Irenaeus, *Against Heresies, Ante-Nicene Fathers: The Writings of the Fathers Down to A.D. 325.* Edited by Alexander Roberts, with James Donaldson and A. Cleveland Coxe. Edinburgh: T&T Clark, 1870.

Josephus, Flavius. *Antiquities of the Jews, The Life and Works of Flavius Josephus.* Translated by William Whiston. Peabody, MA: Hendrickson, nd.

Josephus, Flavius. *Wars of the Jews, The Life and Works of Flavius Josephus.* Translated by William Whiston. Peabody, MA: Hendrickson, nd.

Justin Martyr. *The First Apology, Ante-Nicene Fathers: The Writings of the Fathers Down to A.D. 325.* Edited by Alexander Roberts, with James Donaldson and A. Cleveland Coxe. Edinburgh: T&T Clark, 1870.

Kelly, J.N.D. *Early Christian Doctrines,* 5th edition. London: A & C Black, 1977.

Lake, Kirsopp, trans. *The Apostolic Fathers.* Whitefish MT: Literary Licensing, 2011.

Lanctantius. *The Epitome of the Divine Institutes, Ante-Nicene Fathers: The Writings of the Fathers Down to A.D. 325.* Edited by Alexander Roberts, with James Donaldson and A. Cleveland Coxe. Edinburgh: T&T Clark, 1870.

Lapide, Cornelius A. *The Great Commentary of Cornelius à Lapide.* Translated by Thomas Mossman. London: Hodges, 1896.

Lewis, C.S. *The Essential C.S. Lewis.* Edited by Lyle W. Dorsett. New York: Simon and Schuster, 1996.

Liturgy of the Hours. Totowa, NJ: Catholic Book Publishing, 1975.

Martinez, Florentino Garcia, ed., W.G. Watson, trans. *The Dead Sea Scrolls Translated: The Qumran Texts in English.* Boston: Brill, 1997.

Melito. *Discourse on the Resurrection, in On Pascha and Fragments*. Translated by Stuart George Hall. Oxford: Clarendon Press, 1979.

Mitch, Curtis and Edward Sri. *The Gospel of Matthew: Catholic Commentary on Sacred Scripture*. Grand Rapids: Baker Academic, 2010.

Neusner, Jacob. *Sifra: Aharé mot, Qedoshim, Emor, Behar, and Behuqotai*. Tampa, FL: University of South Florida, 1988.

New Catholic Encyclopedia. New York: McGraw Hill, 1967.

Origen. *Contra Celsum, Ante-Nicene Fathers: The Writings of the Fathers Down to A.D. 325*. Edited by Alexander Roberts, with James Donaldson and A. Cleveland Coxe. Edinburgh: T&T Clark, 1870.

Pausanias. *Description of Greece*. Translated by W. H. Jones and H.A. Ormerod. Boston: Harvard University Press, 1933.

Phillips, John. *Exploring Psalms: An Expository Commentary*, Vol. 1, Grand Rapids, MI: Kregel Academic, 2002.

Pitre, Brant James. *Jesus, the Tribulation, and the End of the Exile: Restoration Eschatology and the Origin of the Atonement*. Grand Rapids, MI: Baker Academic, 2006.

Pliny. *Naturalis Historia: Natural History*. Translated by John F. Healy. London: Penguin Classics, 1991.

Pope Benedict XII. Benedictus Deus: On the Beatific Vision of God. Vatican: Constitution, 1336.

Pope Benedict XVI. *Jesus of Nazareth: From the Baptism in the Jordan to the Transfiguration*. San Francisco, CA: Ignatius Press, 2008.

Pope Benedict XVI. *Jesus of Nazareth: From the Entrance Into Jerusalem To The Resurrection*. San Francisco, CA: Ignatius Press, 2011.

Pope Benedict XVI. *Porta Fidei: Door of Faith*. Vatican: Apostolic Letter, 2011.

Pope Benedict XVI. *Spe Salvi: Saved in Hope.* Vatican: Encyclical Letter, 2007.

Pope John Paul II. "Second Coming at the End of Time." General Audience, April 22, 1998.

Pope Paul III. *Decree Concerning Justification, De Justificatione.* Council of Trent. Vatican, 1547.

Pope Paul VI. *Dogmatic Constitution on Divine Revelation, Dei Verbum:* Second Vatican Council. Vatican, 1965.

Pope Paul VI. *Dogmatic Constitution on the Church, Lumen Gentium:* Second Vatican Council. Vatican, 1964.

Pope Paul VI. *Pastoral Constitution on the Church in the Modern World, Gaudium et Spes:* Second Vatican Council. Vatican, 1965.

Pope Pius IX. *Dogmatic Constitution on the Catholic Faith, Dei Filius:* First Vatican Council. Vatican, 1890.

Pope Pius XI. *Divini Redemptoris: Divine Redeemer.* Vatican: Encyclical, 1937.

Rashi. *Metsudah Chumash Rashi,* Volume 3. Edited by Nachum Y. Kornfeld, Abraham B. Walzer, and Avrohom Davis. Jersey City, NJ: KTAV Publishing House, 1997.

Roberts, Alexander, with James Donaldson and A. Cleveland Coxe, ed. *Ante-Nicene Fathers: The Writings of the Fathers Down to A.D. 325.* Edinburgh: T&T Clark, 1870.

Russell, Bertrand. *Why I Am Not A Christian and Other Essays on Religion and Related Subjects.* Edited by Paul Edward. New York: George Allen & Unwin, 1957.

Schaff, Philip, ed. *Nicene and Post-Nicene Fathers.* Oxford: Parker, 1891.

Schall, James V, S.J. *"The Point of Christianity."* Crisis Magazine, July 18, 2012.

Schmidt, Nathaniel. *Original Language of the Parables of Enoch, Old Testament and Semitic Studies in Memory of William Rainey Harper,* Volume 2. Edited by Robert Francis

Harper, Francis Brown, and George Foot Moore. Chicago, IL: University of Chicago Press, 1908.

Schweitzer, Albert. *The Quest of the Historical Jesus.* Translated by W. Montgomery. London: A & C Black, 1910.

Segelstein, Marcia. *"Courage & Conversion: An Interview with Hadley Arkes." Crisis Magazine,* August 16, 2012.

Skolnik, Fred, ed. *Encyclopaedia Judaica.* Woodbridge, CT: MacMillan Reference, 2007.

Tacitus. *The Annals.* Translated by Alfred John Church and William Jackson Brodribb. Charleston, NC: Nabu Press, 2010.

Tacitus. *The Histories.* Translated by Alfred John Church and William Jackson Brodribb. London: Macmillan, 1927.

Twain, Mark. *Mark Twain in Eruption: Hitherto Unpublished Pages About Men and Events.* Edited by Bernard DeVoto. New York: Harper, 1940.

Wigoder, Geoffrey, ed. *The New Standard Jewish Encyclopedia.* New York: Encyclopedia Publishing Company, 1992.

ABOUT THE AUTHOR

David B. Currie grew up as a preacher's kid in the Fundamentalist movement. After studies at Trinity College and Trinity Evangelical Divinity School, he became a Protestant missionary, but also began investigating theological and biblical questions that he felt had no viable answers in any Protestant tradition. After an often-painful search for the truth, in 1993 he and his family found themselves reluctantly knocking on the door of the Catholic Church—a conversion story that Currie details in his best-selling book, *Born Fundamentalist, Born Again Catholic.*

Currie is also the author of *Rapture: The End-Times Error that Leaves the Bible Behind*, which explores the biblical, historical, and theological roots of the modern Rapture movement. He is a research fellow with the St. Paul Center for Biblical Theology, and has appeared numerous times on radio and television. He and his wife, Colleen, are the parents of eight wonderful children and have been blessed with five beautiful grandchildren.